Wisdom
from the
Angels
and the
Forces of Light

om mani padme hum
pp. 94

Cover Design:

Steve Doolittle

Copyright © 1998 by Astara, Inc.
All Rights Reserved

ISBN 0-918936-33-0

Library of Congress Catalogue Card 98-071940

Printed in the United States of America

Wisdom
from the
Angels
and the
Forces of Light

Earlyne Chaney

Astara's Library of Mystical Classics

Published by

Astara

792 West Arrow Highway
Upland, CA 91785

Other Books by Earlyne Chaney

Remembering—The Autobiography of a Mystic
The Great Work of the Penetralia
Secrets From Mount Shasta
The Book of Beginning Again
Revelations of Things to Come
Beyond Tomorrow—A Book of Prophecies
Shining Moments of a Mystic
Initiation in the Great Pyramid
Forever Young
The You Book—A Treasury of Health and Healing
Lost Secrets of the Mystery Schools
Secret Wisdom of the Great Initiates
The Madonna and the Coming Light
Lost Empire of the Gods

****

Published by Samuel Weiser, Inc.

The Mystery of Death and Dying—
Initiation at the Moment of Death
The Eyes Have It

****

Books in Collaboration

Kundalini and the Third Eye
(With William Messick)
The Mystical Marriage of Science and Spirit
(By Frances Paelian
Based on the teachings of Earlyne Chaney)
Light and Life Cookbook
(With Jan and Alan Pearson)

Dedication and Acknowledgements

The purest of life-giving waters which have filled my own cup now flow over into this book to nourish, sustain, and renew life beyond this vessel. It is in appreciation for what has been given me that this book is dedicated to each of you, with the hope that your search may be somehow enriched through and, in turn, grow beyond these pages.

I most gratefully acknowledge the staunch assistance of my beloved daughter, Sita, and her indispensable role in getting this book to print. It is precious beyond words to see the same deep and abiding love of my Teachers answering her questions and guiding her searches.

I thank, too, my dear assistant and friend, Grace Cooper, who began this project with me, ably and devotedly bringing all the elements together as I moved from one chapter to another.

My deep appreciation also goes to Jeffrey Meyer, Steve Doolittle, Elizabeth Hickerson and Pam Rau, who've brought their individual talents and caring hearts into this effort.

Table of Contents

Preface ix

Chapter 1— Religion and Philosophy 1

Chapter 2 — Work of the Divine Hierarchy 35

Chapter 3 — The Wisdom Teachings in Sacred Texts . . . 55

Chapter 4 — Death and the Soul 65

Chapter 5 — Meditation and Soul Liberation 79

Chapter 6 — Ancient Wisdom 115

Chapter 7 — Holy Nahd 147

Chapter 8 — Psychic Powers 159

Chapter 9 — New Age and Evolution 175

Chapter 10 — Tomorrow-ward 203

Chapter 11 — Spiritual Seeking 219

In Closing 239

Epilogue 241

Preface

Most of the years of my adult life have been spent communicating with forces beyond the realm of human vision. During my years as a mystical teacher and writer, one of my activities was to hold seminars called Satsangs. A Satsang is a meeting where seekers of New Age wisdom come together to ask questions of a teacher concerning various topics of Ancient Wisdom. A Satsang, then, is a question-answer seminar.

Those attending my Satsangs were asked to write their questions on slips of paper, which were then brought to me for answering. I enjoyed these seminars because they brought me into closer contact with New Age seekers, and also because they required no prior preparation on my part. I simply turned the answering over to my spirit Teachers, guides and Angels, who channeled answers through to my consciousness.

The questions in this publication have been selected from those most frequently asked at these Satsangs — which explains why there may occasionally appear some measure of repetition.

Since humankind first appeared on this planet, there have been questions concerning the soul and human destiny. It is therefore hoped that those unseen Teachers who have sought to answer these questions have tapped into the secrets of the Universe to share their enlightenment.

This book is released with a prayer that it point the readers toward further Light on their paths of soul progression.

Earlyne C. Chaney
Upland, California

Chapter I

Religion and Philosophy

QUESTION: What is God?

ANSWER: To the Christian and Jew, the word God in its singular form involves the highest manifestation of absolute Deity, embracing within itself all other gods and energies. This word comes from the ancient Hebrew Yod, or Jod. But as the Hebrew Yod, this symbolic term only represented the creator of physical humanity on the lower planes. It had nothing to do with the creation or formation of spirit, and has nothing to do with the triple Deity: Father, Son and Holy Ghost — or Cosmos, Chaos and Theos — which involves all.

We accept the principle of the one God of the monotheist while we deny Him/Her as being anthropomorphic, or possessing only human attributes. But we embrace the divine principle in nature. The absolute Deity has to be unconditioned and unrelated. Any Deity or Divine Being that manifests in time and space can be but a fractional part of the whole. Therefore, the active creating gods must be but mere aspects of the All. The cosmic theory has to start with the divine primordial substance diffused throughout boundless space, possessing both divinity and mind. It is this plane of substance radiating in the highest boundaries of the universe that we call the Godhead. This is representative of God, but it is not God. It is only the highest form of an infinitely evolving entity that we can perceive. It is out of this celestial substance, clothing itself in various forms of denser qualities, that the planes of the universe are formed.

This one principle is not the immediate creator of the visible universe. It is on the sixth plane, the Monadic plane rising out of the Godhead, that God becomes "the gods." It is on this divine plane that the creators, the planners and the architects come forth, for this is the manifested plane of being. This plane is the primeval reflection of the formless Cause. This is also the plane of the Christ Substance, the son of the Father-Mother primordial substance of the Godhead.

On this Monadic plane are the first primordial seven — in Christianity they are the archangels. These same beings are called by other names in other faiths and religions. They are the Seven Lights before the Throne; they are the Rays, or First Emanation of the eternally self-existent One. They have proceeded out of the Father-Mother Godhead. From these First primordial Seven came subsequently the Seven Builders. These Seven Builders became the seven creative contractors following the blueprints of the first primordial Seven Architects. Following these blueprints, the Seven Builders created the lower worlds.

The hierarchy of spiritual beings which extends from the Earth to the highest known spiritual planes, consists of souls who have lived on Earth — or some other material planet — and have progressed through eons of evolution to attain union with the higher planes. They extend like the angels on Jacob's Ladder, from Earth through these planes. This hierarchy — like a vast army — indeed forever treads up and down the ladder, and is composed of various groupings led by beings which vary by evolved states of consciousness.

Religion and Philosophy

The purpose of this spiritual hierarchy is to guide the evolution of humanity from Earth to the Godhead.

Every seeker's concept of God differs according to the image within his/her own soul. For one's soul is nothing but a convex mirror of one's perceptions. In that convex mirror of your soul, you see your individual God. If the reflection is clear, a divine image will shine like the noonday sun. If the mirror is clouded, one may declare there is no God, for God for such a one will be obscured. His/her mirror will be misted over, and because they cannot find their God, either within themselves or in any of their outer manifestations and handiwork, he/she is apt to declare that there is no God, or that their God is dead.

But the one who declares that there is no God must presume that there is no soul. If there is no God and no soul, then both the planet and the humanity that has inherited the planet goes floating onward in a circle of eternal blindness, under no divine jurisdiction, and under no divine cause. The Earth and its humanity, then, goes hurtling through space toward no particular destiny, headed for nothingness. Such a concept is, to the mystic, a horrendous nightmare. You cannot be a "no-thing." You cannot be the product of a cosmic accident — the effect of a causeless cause.

QUESTION: What can one say to an atheist to prove the existence of God?

ANSWER: The ancient scriptures — the Upanishads and the Rig-Veda — refer to the fivefold substances of creation, including both the Earth and human beings.

First, there is the realm of matter ensouled by the lifeforce which, in turn, is embraced by the mental substance, which is overshadowed by the realms of Truth (Light). All of these live and move and have their being out of the great bosom of the First Cause, the Godhead, Bliss.

Thus we list the fivefold ladder of being, all manifesting in our world of duality, but not all understood:
1. Matter
2. Life
3. Mind
4. Truth (Light)
5. Bliss

When we refer to the mystic formula of earth, water, air, fire and Azoth — or when we refer to initiation by earth, fire, air and water — the earth of the mystic formula refers to the realm of matter. It is only a symbolic term for the principles of matter, the atomic structure of matter.

To use "earth" in describing the mystic formula is somewhat confusing. It would be more readily understood were we to say that we refer to the realm of matter — the material substance which creates the entire sidereal kingdom and not the substance we call earth — a substance which is solid and tangible and responsive to the senses — a substance upon which we can build our world and base our operations.

Does not the existence of substance ranging from matter to spirit suggest the implication that your physical body, being chemically arranged in a formula of solids, liquids and gasses, might be rearranged in a less chemical formula? Is it not possible that we might follow Paul's injunction to "stir up the gift of God within us," thereby changing the formula of the physical form?

If we truly looked to the Master Jesus as an Avatar worthy of emulating might not we, too, embrace the science of the transfiguration as a part of our own evolution? Under the power of transmutation, his physical form was transfigured and became luminous with light and shone like the sun. Might not we, too, learn that secret process of transmutation? Might this not be the secret of the great liberation sought in all the Mystery Schools of the past?

Even when we consider the world of matter-duality, we deal with gradations of substance — from the subtle gasses and ethers to the dense and gross physical.

Pondering as to what causes the mysterious operations of being behind the substances of matter, might not science discover the workings of spirit? What mysterious force lies behind the highest gradation of physical substance? Surely, not a great nothing — an unfathomable void — for neither science nor God recognizes a void. What seems to be void is only the realm beyond the grasp of our five senses.

If the brain is not the creator of thought — and obviously it is not — then, what substance or what power created the brain? Since the brain itself is the thing created and the instrument employed, its very existence implies the presence of a Creator or a Universal Mind.

Thus, we can explain to the atheist, we come abruptly face to face with the obvious existence of a higher substance than matter. For the mind must be created of a substance intangible and undiscoverable by the five senses.

One could more easily agree with the atheist in declaring there is no God and no force beyond this material existence, except that would be to negate the obvious — which is that the material world is only the effect of an unseen cause — a result or the extension of an obvious, more subtle form of substance and force.

To declare that the material world begins and ends with its compound of chemical substances, its gasses, its physical forces, would seem a simple matter. But one is immediately faced with involved enigmas and questions.

To posit a world of matter and cut it off from its source of supply is like the Hindu rope trick — tossing the rope into the air and expecting it to stand there alone and unaided by any other outside force. The world of matter would collapse upon itself without the nourishment and substance from other spheres.

Fortunately, the evolution of the forces of life, mind and soul out of the imprisonment of matter is not left up to the human race. In his biblical writings, Paul constantly refers to "a new heaven and a new Earth and a new man." Earth of itself will evolve into an etheric existence, according to the pressure applied upon the dense atoms from the superior planes which surround it. This, coupled with its gradual movement into the ethers of a new age, will automatically result in an immortalization of the dense physical Earth and humanity's dense form.

That ye put off, concerning the former conversation, the old man, which is corrupt according to the deceitful lusts; And be renewed in the spirit of your mind; And that ye put on the new man, which after God is created in righteousness and true holiness.

Ephesians 4:22-24

And if Christ be in you, the body is dead because of sin; but the Spirit is life because of righteousness.... The Spirit itself beareth witness with our spirit, that we are children of God. And if children, then heirs; heirs of God, and joint-heirs with Christ.

Romans 8: 10, 16-17

Let it not be thought that, in seeking to conquer death, we glorify earthly immortality or attach an undue sense of importance to the corporeal form. The form in its present limited capacity is indeed abhorrent to all that is desired by the spirit. It is toward the immortal flesh that we tend — life in a body fit to be inhabited by a god — and an earth plane fit to be called a paradise.

QUESTION: You say the rise of Christianity caused the fall of the Mystery Schools. Could you be more specific and perhaps give an example?

ANSWER: The best example could concern Julian, the initiate emperor of Rome.

Julian, called the Apostate, was born and raised a pagan, acquainted with the Mysteries and initiation. During his youth he was persuaded toward the Christian faith, but accepted it only on the surface to save his life. He was well acquainted with the punishment accorded those who refused to convert to Christianity. Later in life, however, he turned again toward the Mysteries and, while in the city of Ephesus, received his initiation into the Order of the Mother of the Gods, which took place in the subterranean chambers beneath the temple of Artemis. This temple was only one of a vast complex of buildings at Ephesus which composed the sanctuary of Artemis, later renamed Diana by the Romans.

Julian was persuaded toward this initiation by the aged and venerable Maximus, who was the Ephesian master of the Neo-Platonic School in the city of Pergamos. He was also a celebrated adept in the secret science of theurgy and true magic. Edesius of Pergamos, who presided over the Neo-Platonic

School, introduced Julian to the elderly Maximus. At the time, Julian was studying with Eusebius, the renowned Christian historian, at Pergamos near Ephesus. Pergamos was also called Pergamum or Pergamus. Today it is known as Bergama.

At a gathering of many Christian leaders, Maximus, high priest of Hellenic Mystery Schools, reminded Eusebius of the time when Eusebius had invited some Christian friends to the temple of Artemis to witness Maximus, during a ceremony, burning incense and chanting a hymn before the statue of Artemis. He further reminded Eusebius how amazed they had been to see the statue of the goddess suddenly smile and laugh aloud. Maximus had calmed them by requesting that they watch closely since the torches she held were about to burst into flame. Immediately afterward they did.

Eusebius was convinced that, hearing Maximus tell of this "pagan" ceremony, Julian would no longer be curious about Maximus and his magical science, and would forever turn away from the Mysteries and totally embrace Christianity. The exact opposite occurred. Hearing of this amazing happening caused Julian to conclude his studies with Eusebius and seek Maximus as his teacher. Julian was familiar with the Nicene Council presided over by Eusebius and the Emperor Constantine, his uncle, in 325 A.D. He was aware of the quarrel which had raged among the 318 bishops attending the council as to which of the numerous canonical gospels would be selected to compose the Holy Bible, the "Word of God."

Being unable to decide which books of the inspired gospels to choose, it was decided to leave the decision to divine intervention. The plan was to place all the books of the gospels under a communion table in the council chamber and leave them overnight. During the night the bishops were to pray that the Lord himself would place the chosen gospels on top of the table,

Religion and Philosophy   9

while the rejected ones were to remain underneath. The plan worked admirably — strange coincidence how the very books favored by Constantine were the books the Lord chose. But no one has ever questioned as to which of the bishops held the keys to the council chamber, and thus had access during the night to the communion table and the gospels.

Julian never questioned but that it was Constantine the Emperor, Sabinus the bishop of Heraclea, and Eusebius who held the keys. But for this same type of divination — divine intervention — the Church subsequently labeled all such practitioners heathens, magicians and witches, and burnt them by the hundreds at the stake — including the divine Joan of Arc who, hundreds of years after Constantine's reign, refused to recant that she heard the voices of the saints speaking to her, guiding her toward victory in battle. For "listening to the voices of the saints" she was burnt at the stake.

No less a tragedy befell the beautiful and learned Hypatia, who expounded the doctrines of the divine Plato, Pythagoras and Plotinus, in her academy at Rome. She had studied under Plutarch, head of the Athenian school, and was learned in all the secrets of theurgy — thus she spoke openly, contending that all miracles must be judged non-miraculous if natural causes could be produced by which they might occur. She also talked openly of how "the Word of God" — the gospels of the Bible — had been "divined" at the Nicene Council.

Hypatia, even during her lifetime, was acclaimed as the most wise of womankind. She was the daughter of the great Greek astronomer and mathematician, Theon of Alexandria, Egypt. In the prime of her earthly life she was universally admired for her great learning, talents, elegance, beauty and modesty. She exercised marvelous influence over all who heard her public utterances. Each day before her academy stood a long train of chariots. Her lecture room was crowded with the wealthy and fashionable of Alexandria. They came to listen to her discourses on the great questions which humankind in all ages has asked; "What am I? Where am I? What can I do? Where am I going? Where have I come from?"

It was Cyril, Archbishop of Alexandria, who ordered her death and released a mob of Christian zealots to attack her chariot as she drove on the streets of Rome, dragging her from her chariot and committing her murder. She was stripped naked in the streets, dragged into a church and there slain with a club. Her body was cut into pieces. The flesh was scraped from the bone with shells and the remnants cast into a fire. Archbishop Cyril was never held accountable for this crime. He continued to reign as a high official in the church of that day.

But back to Julian. After being initiated by Maximus into the Ephesian Mysteries, Julian was also introduced to many mystical practices, including midnight worship or rites to the goddess Artemis. Maximus also introduced Julian to the concept of reincarnation as taught by the Pythagoreans. He further convinced Julian that he was overshadowed by the soul of Alexander the Great and, as such, was destined to conquer the world. At Ephesus, Julian completed a full course of studies in magic and the esoteric and mystical arts.

Julian dared not speak of his mystical activities, knowing full well that his uncle, the new Emperor Constantine, having embraced Christianity as the state's official religion, and having murdered three of his own sons for refusing to convert to Christianity, would have him put to death. He continued lip service to Christianity. He became Roman Emperor on Constantine's death in 362. His first act was to reopen all the pagan temples — Ephesus, Eleusis, Delphi.

Religion and Philosophy

Secretly, he recognized the emerging doctrines of Christianity to be the Ancient Wisdom stripped of its true depth and truths. Rather than witness the total loss of the Mysteries, he was instrumental in seeing much of the Mystery wisdom integrated into Christianity as exoteric doctrine, not mystical concepts. He has been painted as a monstrous ogre who sought to bring back "the gods and idols of heathenism." The Church has forever stamped him as a "pagan," which labeled him as one "against Christianity, the Apostate." Actually, Julian was not attempting to destroy Christianity but only to restore the Mystery Schools.

Taking Julian's viewpoint, he probably sought initiation in the Mysteries partly because of his hatred for his uncle, Constantine, who had not only murdered the closest members of his family, but many others who refused to convert to Christianity. Nor did Julian look with favor upon Eusebius, who forever stamped the mystery teachings with innumerable oversights when, out of ignorance, he translated them into Christian dogma. Although Eusebius was familiar with the secret doctrines and manuscripts of the Mysteries, he was not learned in them, and did not understand the full implication of their truths.

And so it was with ignorance and half-truths that the Mysteries were rewritten and introduced as twisted Christian dogmas — such as the resurrection of the physical body which, Eusebius declared, would rise up from the grave at the far-distant final Judgment Day, a dogma which emphatically refuted the teaching of reincarnation. Julian knew well it was the soul, not the body, which would be resurrected, not on the "last Judgment Day," but immediately after death. Christianity embraced the dogma of Eusebius and does so still today.

Nearly 700 years B.C., in the schools of both Thales and Pythagoras, great philosophers taught the globular form of Earth and its journey around the sun, along with the planets of the solar system. Yet in 317 A.D. Lactantius, the converted son of Constantine the Great, taught that the Earth was a plane surrounded by the sky, composed of fire and water. He warned all the new Christians against accepting the "heretical" doctrine of the Earth as a globe. Thus Julian was well aware that he must compare the infantile teachings of Lactantius against the noble knowledge of the great Pythagoras of Samos — and he chose the way of the Samean philosopher.

An arrow shot into Julian's chest put an inglorious end to the young emperor's magnificent effort to lift the Roman government out of political corruption by means of far-reaching and statesman-like reforms. He had attempted Plato's doctrine that the state should be ruled by philosophers. But his reign was cut short after less than two years of incomparable progress, and thus ended the life of a profound scholar and a genuine lover of great Greek esoteric wisdom.

It was not his purpose to restore pagan "superstition." His purpose was to restore philosophical understanding and, indeed, to end superstition, whether it be called pagan or Christian. He sought to bring understanding of the Mystery religions. He was aware that the worship of the gods had drifted lamentably from the grasp of the lofty principles of true spiritual science and mystical knowledge. These alone could lend sound meaning to the rituals and symbolic representations of the old religion which Rome had inherited. He sought to revise the Mysteries of previous years with their deeper esoteric input, including the concept of reincarnation.

His early death should be mourned even today as one of the most fatal losses in all history. He most certainly would have reestablished the Greek academies, such as that of Plato, in an attempt to reeducate an intelligentsia in the esoteric background of the Mystery religious rites and symbols. Such a restoration would have offered early Christianity a strong foundation. Realizing that the old Mystery dramas had been degraded, Eusebius sought to lift the Eucharist of Dionysus, which had become nothing more than a drunken debauchery, and other dramas to their former glory.

What must have been his saddened thoughts when viewing the world as a young emperor? He saw the degradation on both sides — that of the old esoteric Mystery initiations and the frenzied efforts of Christianity to convert the followers of the Mysteries. He was attempting to establish a firm foundation beneath both movements when his life ended. It is difficult to contemplate the destiny of the human race had his life extended for the usual seventy years.

Gregory, one of the early Church founders, writing after Julian's death, relentlessly thrust the soul of Julian into hell while simultaneously summoning from heaven the soul of Constantine, whom he called "the most devout and Christ-loving of emperors." This is the way he described the murdering leader, heaping him with praise — while heaping Julian with infamy. On his deathbed Julian uttered a prophecy that "the Galilean will eventually conquer" — meaning that Jesus, the Galilean, would eventually triumph in spite of the doctrines and dogmas of the expanding Church.

And in spite of the misconceptions and mistranslation of his teachings by Eusebius and the early Church fathers. Only by true seekers can Julian's early death be recognized as an infinite tragedy, and only time will tell how the mystical teachings of the noble Galilean, and other great Avatars, will eventually triumph.

QUESTION: Can you explain more fully how much of Christianity was, and is, based upon the secret doctrines of the Mystery Schools?

ANSWER: On the surface it appears that Western Christianity went to great lengths to rid the world of "pagan gods," but what is least understood is how the early Christian fathers absorbed into their infant religion the pagan gods themselves. Unable to expel them, they often made them into undesirable spirits, or bestowed their benign qualities upon their own saints and angels. The Christian fathers, and the earlier Hebrew religionists, did not so much consider the old pagan gods as evil as they considered their own One God to be superior. They sought to establish that whatever the pagan religions did for their followers, the religion of Jehovah or Jesus could do better.

The absorption of the early gods and their functions into the realm of Christianity was known as Theokracia. Gentle persuasion was the attempted process, but more than once force was applied, not only by the priesthood, but by the emperors and conquerors themselves. All during the decades of Theokracia, when gentle persuasion was not effective, no torture was too severe, no repression too persistent for the Church to employ in its effort to "save souls." There was no hesitancy to burn at the stake not only the backslider who sought to return once more to the old faith, but as a means of convincing those of the resistance.

When the pagan gods could not be depicted as evil entities, they were portrayed as symbols, as energies, as forces embracing the psychic, somatic and intellectual human personality. But their detractors' first step toward persuasion was to make devils out of the ancient gods. Thus, any contact with them, or worship of them, was labeled as sinful — as being "the work of

Religion and Philosophy 15

the devil." Such efforts often failed, however. Many of the mythological names survived. The first three centuries of Christianity marked the transitional period between Judeo-Christian faith and paganism.

It comes as a startling surprise to discover that organized Christianity would be empty indeed, and perhaps would never have survived as a major religion had it not lifted from the Mystery Schools many of its traditions. It may be of interest to cite some of these instances.

First of all, we must realize that during the time of Jesus, his teachings had scarcely filtered beyond the boundaries of Palestine itself. Although he spoke to many thousands, most were curiosity seekers, or those seeking to be healed. The majority turned quickly away to return to their organized Judaism or other beliefs, looking upon the Master simply as another prophet, of which there had been many in Israel. Organized Judaism had been following its traditions for countless centuries and clearly was not disposed to accept a new variation. In Rome and Greece the gods of Olympus were firmly established in religious thought. Hindu customs and beliefs were age-old and unimpressed by current changes. To the south, Egypt, in her impressive dignity, was beyond influence.

Thus, the teachings of the man of Galilee created scarcely a ripple on the religious surface of the age. It became a recognized religion only because the disciples, urged by the words of their ascended Master, traveled throughout the known world, perpetuating the teachings which had been left in their keeping.

Paul, the leading organizer, founded the theological system which has prevailed even to the present time. The early Church fathers, therefore, were faced with the most diligent dilemma — endeavoring to establish a new faith in a land already torn asunder between several well established hereditary traditions. It is interesting to observe how they overcame these difficulties, adjusting their teachings and dogmas to the principles already firmly established and accepted by the existing faiths, especially the precepts of the Mystery Schools.

Remember also that Jesus himself was a student of the Ancient Mystery Schools. Through his teachings he sought to bring the mystical ideas of Self-realization, reincarnation, karma, and the divine attributes present in every soul to the masses. He was not advocating an end to the Mystery Schools, but rather encouraging an awakening of each person to their divine potential through meditation, prayer, love and service.

QUESTION: Again, can you give specific examples?

ANSWER: The Mysteries of Mithras could be among the foremost of those woven into early Christianity.

The worshippers of Mithras believed him to be a god of light, solar and spiritual, and consequently Mysteries of his would constitute enlightenment. For 1200 years Mithraism was the official religion of the Persian kingdom. It spread throughout surrounding countries and even Romans embraced it. Mithraism, preceding Christianity, presented the cross, the priestly robes, the symbols, the sacraments, the Sabbath, the festivals and the anniversaries which are now celebrated by the Christian faith.

Mithraism practiced a baptism and holy communion as a part of their initiation. Its similarity to Christianity was astonishing. So much so that Tertullian, a spokesman for Christianity, claimed Mithraism had been "invented by the devil" for the purpose of counterfeiting Christianity. Rome strove zealously to establish that Mithraism was patterned after Christianity, but such claims were met with incredulity, since even the peasantry knew that Mithraism preceded Christianity by at least 500 years.

Every important feast day of the organized Church, including the Church of England, falls upon days that have long been remembered for their association with certain pagan gods. The greatest feast day of Artemis-Diana became the festival of the Assumption in organized Christianity. The festival of St. George was originally celebrated in honor of Parilia, for example.

The birth of Mithras was celebrated on what is now equivalent to the twenty-fifth day of December. He was a tremendously popular deity, and his birth was observed as a festival in a wide area, including Syria and Egypt. This was the same day which marked the birth of the sun in the pagan religion. So, being unable to establish an equally important day and, reckoning this day as the day of the winter solstice, in 375 A.D. the Church at Antioch officially fixed the 25th of December as the date of Christ's nativity.

By accepting the winter solstice as the birth date of Jesus, the Church fathers immediately embraced the followers of Mithras, who would then more readily accept the teachings of the Christian faith. In the beginning, the Church fathers had attempted to establish the 6th day of January as the birthday of Jesus. January 6th became the Epiphany, which it remains even now in Western Christian tradition.

And what of Easter? During the days of antiquity, the death of the Greek god Adonis was celebrated in Spring, usually on what is now the 24th and 25th of March. The ancient Greeks celebrated not only the death of Adonis, but his subsequent resurrection. And many nature-based and Goddess religions celebrated the Spring Equinox, around what is now March 20, as a time of rebirth. The Church accordingly adopted this season to coincide with the crucifixion and resurrection of Jesus. There is an historical basis, as well, for this Christian celebration being observed in spring, since Jesus was crucified during the holy days of Passover, which fall at the time of the Paschal moon, a variable event which may occur in any of the months of spring.

As we approach the dawn of the Aquarian Age another such transition is occurring, that is, the Judeo-Christian ethos and the new Aquarian Age. Once again the long suppressed basic instincts of the human race are reasserting themselves — now appearing in free expression. The universal hunger of the soul for greater knowledge, greater wisdom and for Self-realization is a definite "sign of the times."

The first evidence of this break away from crystallized tradition was the sexual revolution, the civil rights movement and the women's movement. Once it has swept through the world it will again become stabilized. But having once tasted freedom from the yoke of dogma, the New Age souls will again turn to the Mystery Schools, the old compassionate gods and goddesses, and initiation — as a means of Self-realization and soul progression.

Incoming souls will bound forward in their reaching toward a new-found God. For Christians the god-man Jesus will assume an even greater savior image as his mother, the divine Virgin, assumes her equal place by his side, thus balancing the positive-negative polarities toward which human beings are ever evolving.

Until now, because the neophyte has been influenced by the orthodox Christian tendencies, he/she has had little opportunity to overcome a natural prejudice against earlier religions and their gods, deities and goddesses because conventional

Christianity tends to present them in a greatly distorted light. It is important then to probe deeply into paganism to discover how it differs from Christianity.

First of all, the word was created by the early Christian fathers to elevate their personal theology above previous religious principles by classifying, in a derogatory manner, all religious thought that did not follow in the channels of conventional Church theology. The word "pagan" is a Latin derivative coming from two words. First, "paganus," meaning civilian, or peasant. Second, "pagus" meaning village or outlying district. Thus the true sense of pagans is, "those who are living outside the boundaries of an established site."

In ancient days those Christians living inside the cities worshipped in groups that had accepted the ecclesiastical standards established by Paul, who was himself a city dweller. They eventually came to regard themselves as quite different from the paganus, or rural dwellers — those outside city walls who rarely came in contact with Christian precepts. Many of the country people continued to follow the religious worship and traditions of their Olympian gods, or the matriarchal tradition of Goddess and nature worship. It followed naturally then that Christianity gradually became associated with culture, whereas paganism came to represent those beliefs that were not embraced by this "new" and illuminating teaching.

The distinction between orthodox religion and paganism was the result of the organized Church which, incidentally, did not come to be such until centuries after the death of the Master. In this sense the Master himself would be classified as a pagan, for he constantly escaped the confines of the city to teach in the fields, by the river's edge, in the forests and in the wilderness, even on the mountaintop. He sought the paganus for his disciples, and his greatest teachings and works were performed for them — the "heathen." From such a pagan religion have come all the great teachers of the past, including Jesus himself, Plato, Socrates, Aristotle, Buddha, Pythagoras, Apollonius, the followers of the Goddess tradition in many cultures, and all those to whom the Christian orthodox church was an unknown entity. In this sense then, those who have sought beyond traditional Christianity could ourselves be called pagans.

In the initiations of the Mysteries, the hierophants sought to approach an approximation of the god form so that, through this association, they might apprehend and share with their initiates the better understanding of their esoteric development. We cannot separate ourselves from the past, from that which we have called paganism. If the light is to come to Earth we must open our consciousness more and more to the direct mystical teachings that gave life, identity and purpose to pagan initiations. Presently, it is usually only the light seeker that strives to recapture something of the pagan's magical support, to find God in the ever present now, discover cosmic power in the manifestations of nature which abound around us, and attempt to realize the union between the Logos and humankind.

Christian theology owes much to paganism. A religion or philosophy which can develop a Plato, a Mary, a Plutarch, an Apollonius, an Isis, a Pythagoras, a Socrates, is not gross, superficial or totally unworthy of our deepest consideration. We have entered the stages of initiation, and reaching into the Mysteries and truths of the past helps us form the future of our spiritual progress. This is ordination into the cosmic priesthood — of which Jesus, a priest of Melchizedek, is leader. As Julian said, "the Galilean will eventually triumph" as Aquarian Age seekers strive to enfold in a New Age philosophy the truths Jesus really taught.

Religion and Philosophy

QUESTION: In many of the Schools it was the Goddess who dominated the initiation and acted as hierophant. Could you speak of some of the forms of the Goddess?

ANSWER: "Mother Nature" has become so common an expression we use it frequently without pausing to consider that it embraces the gods and goddesses of long ago, as well as the symbology of their powers. Mother Nature symbolizes Earth itself — negative-feminine in polarity — as opposed to the masculine-positive sun. Several of the most important of the goddesses were recognized as Great Earth Mothers. Among the most prominent of these goddesses were Athena, Astarte, Isis, Ishtar, Demeter and Artemis.

In other writings I have spoken at length concerning the Mysteries of Eleusis and Ephesus, which embraced the mystery of Demeter and her daughter, Persephone. I have described how Demeter, in her wrath following the abduction of her daughter Persephone by Hades, Lord of the underworld, caused the harvest on the Earth to cease.* There was no fruit, no corn, no wheat, no agricultural growth of any kind. No seeds yielded their harvest. This persisted until all humankind was threatened with starvation. Only then was Persephone released to spend eight months each year with her mother on Mt. Olympus. Four months of the year — the months of winter — were spent below with Hades. After achieving this victory, Demeter permitted the Earth to "grow" again.

Astarte is another of the Great Earth goddesses. She was recognized in her temples as the Mother of Creation. During her prominence it was customary for all young maidens to serve

* See: *Lost Secrets of the Mystery Schools* by E. Chaney. (Published by Astara, P.O. Box 5003, Upland, CA. 91785.)

in her temples for a certain period of time prior to marriage. This custom was universal throughout Greece and Syria. None were excused from this obligation, from the lowest to the highest families. In Armenia, however, only maidens from the highest families were dedicated to this service.

In Egypt, Isis was known as the Corn Goddess. Reapers gathered in her temples at harvest time to conduct a ritual asking forgiveness for slaying the corn by cutting the stalks. During these festivities she was called the "creator of growing things" and "the lady of abundance." Isis was worshipped not only in Egypt, but in Rome.

The worship of Isis in its formal aspects persisted in Rome, even during the years of the fall of the empire, its depression and decay. Her temple remained the center of moral and spiritual stability during times of chaos. Ceremonies honoring Isis adopted a highly symbolical form — marked baptisms, processionals, festivities at dawn, noon and evening — all of which were systematically regulated by ordained priests of the Order of Isis. Isis was often depicted with the infant Horus on her knees. In the Catholic Church, even today, the Virgin Mary is pictured in remarkably similar aspects, holding the infant Jesus upon her knees.

Many were the temples in ancient days dedicated to the Goddess. Some of these temples were Mystery Schools in their own right. The high priestesses and priests of these temples initiated seekers during elaborate ceremonies in which initiates dedicated themselves to the mystery teachings and the unfolding of that particular feminine aspect which each Goddess represented, such as love, compassion, or creativity. From this ancient tradition we can still see the divine feminine represented in the major religions and spiritual movements of today.

Here are just a few of the goddesses and the symbols which

came to represent the feminine aspect of the Divine: Mother Earth, the moon, the sea, Kwan Yin in the Far East, the Virgin Mary in the West, Isis, Hathor and Maat in Egypt, the forest, the lion, the cow, the snake, Ninhursag and Inanna in Sumer, Ishtar in Babylon and Purga in India, the Tree of Life, Gaia of Ancient Greece, the Shekinah of Judaism, and many more. All had their beginnings in the Ancient Goddess religions which were, like the Mystery Schools, dealt a terrible blow by the patriarchal influences in all traditional religions, influences which went against the equality and the inherent balance between male and female principles taught by the Avatars of the religions, including Jesus.

QUESTION: Can you explain the symbol of the caduceus as it relates to the Mystery Schools?

ANSWER: One of the most subtle of the ancient symbols is that of the caduceus, with its two entwining serpents. In this symbol lies the great twofold wisdom of the gods themselves. The symbol contains male and female potencies. The male aspect involves the development and the attainment of initiation — a positive aspect of force, the pingala. This male-positive serpent represents the accumulation of wisdom and the attainment of knowledge. But wisdom must be polarized in expression through the female or negative quality, the ida. The initiate who absorbs knowledge, who deepens his/her understanding, is like a pool of water that continues to absorb more and more moisture. But without the underlying love currents of the female polarity, it becomes a stagnant pool.

On the other hand, we have the shallow, wild brook that races madly over hill and dale creating much babbling and covering great distances. But it soon exhausts itself and loses its identity by merging into a great river. This symbolizes initiates who are always busy attaining progression through service, but who never find time to increase their knowledge or wisdom through meditation or study. Such acts of service, though always appreciated and of benefit, seldom reward the initiate with an innate wisdom. The caduceus represents a fusion of these two.

Even as it also represents the ida and pingala nerves rising and crossing at the chakras in the spine, it still represents the pathway trod by the wise initiate, melding both service and wisdom, which marks the adept. Such an adept ascends toward liberation, represented by the globe with the outspread wings, atop the caduceus.

Throughout mythology the symbol of the serpent and the Goddess is repeated. Such a symbol embraces great cosmic forces and their association with individual consciousness. One constantly meets the moon goddess with the serpent at her feet, who, taking the seeking soul by the hand, gently leads it into the divine presence of the great wisdom gods, represented often by Hermes, Thoth and Osiris. It is the development of all faculties through the proper balancing of these powers of mind that true wisdom is attained. The pathway of the initiate is one involving both wisdom and love to give it — the soul — its highest and initiatory attainment.

QUESTION: Because the truths presented by the Mystery Schools were so profound, and because many of the Schools had become corrupt, is it possible there were divine forces at work to see that the truths became integrated into the new religion of Christianity, even in their exoteric form, so that these truths and ceremonies did not become altogether extinct from human knowledge and future soul progression?

ANSWER: Contemplating the direct absorption of the esoteric mysteries of the Mystery Schools into the newly created Christianity, at first we are tempted to consider this simply an accidental duplication, a lack of originality, a direct copying of that which has gone before. But then comes a realization that the great truths of the cosmos and the hierarchy must be carried forward for the spiritual progression of the soul, regardless the title under which it shines, whether it be "Mystery School" or "Christianity."

Was there, indeed, some overshadowing power, force or intelligence which caused this repetition of the Mystery Schools, even in exoteric form, to move into Christianity for the fulfillment and progression of the soul, and which directs its operation and use? We can find some measure of an answer in the identity of the Oversoul. Searching for the best possible definition of the Oversoul and its nature we turn to Emerson in his essay of the same title — *The Oversoul:*

"The supreme critic on the errors of the past and the present, and the only prophet of that which might be, is the great nature in which we rest, as the Earth lies in the soft arms of the atmosphere; that unity, that Oversoul, in which every man's particular being is contained and made one with all other; that common heart, of which all sincere conversation is the worship, to which all right action is submissive; that overpowering reality which confutes our tricks and talents, and constrains everyone to pass for what he is, and to speak from his character, and not from his tongue, and which evermore tends to pass into our thought and hand, and become wisdom, and virtue, and power, and beauty. We live in succession, in division, in part, in particles. Meantime within man is the soul of the whole; the wise silence; the universal beauty, to which every part and particle is equally related — the eternal One."

This helps us to understand a measure of the individual Oversoul — but could there be a Universal Oversoul, a guiding deity that stimulates the spiritual aspirations of humankind and which caused the founders of Christianity to seek to absorb the truths of the Mysteries so that they would not be eternally lost to the evolution of humankind? Had the Church fathers not absorbed these secrets of initiation — including the rites of communion, the Holy Virgin as the Earth Mother, the rite of Holy Eucharist — and made them exoteric to the common Christian, Christianity may have fallen by the wayside. Because the soul ever seeks to be illumined by a reflection of some overshadowing Absolute Deity, throughout all the ages humanity has felt the desire to give homage to powers beyond itself. Each race and each age has built the image of that Deity to the best of its understanding and every age has seen each race united by an intangible bond to that Absolute Deity.

The limitation of human understanding causes us to confuse the shadow with the substance. It must have been the eternal influence of the Cosmic Oversoul that has caused the soul to seek ceaselessly and relentlessly for the unchanging reality which instinctively it realizes exists. While we turned to Emerson to quote an enlightening definition of the Oversoul, had Emerson likewise turned to Plotinus who, sixteen hundred years prior to Emerson, defined the Oversoul? Plotinus said:

"First let every soul consider what is the World Soul which created all things, breathing into them the breath of life — into all living things that are on earth, in the air, and in the sea, and the stars in heaven, the sun, and the great heaven itself. The creative World Soul sets them in their order and directs their

Religion and Philosophy

motions, keeping Itself apart from the things which It orders, and moves, and causes to live."

In other words, Plotinus teaches that this World Soul is a form of creative energy. He pictures that it is in this World Soul that the Earth soul, the sun soul and the star soul are born and exist. He also pictured that while the World Soul is the host to these lesser, but divine souls, it nevertheless is separate and apart from them.

Christianity has taught of this World Soul in the form of the Trinity — Father, Son, and Holy Ghost. The ancient Kabbalah taught of this supernal triad in Kether, Chokmah and Binah. Did the early Church fathers dip into the secrets of the Kabbalah to establish their supernal triad? They taught of this supernal triad as the first manifestation of the great unmanifest, the pure Absolute. The Kabbalah called it the Ain. Out of Ain came the creative energy, the basis of all existence. But even as it is the source of creation, it is restrained and set apart from manifestation.

Eternally connected with the Trinity, or Ain, the Godhead, the consciousness, subconsciousness, or superconsciousness continually seeks its source, drawn to it by an irresistible force of magnetic attraction. But the soul is met with an opposing force we recognize as karma, both world karma and individual, built into the character, environment, circumstances and similar influences.

It is this karmic pattern which causes the soul to travel to its ultimate goal of illumination through a series of wide and circuitous detours. It is the unchanging, eternal World Soul, however, where the point of all evolutionary development converges. Within this indomitable force all hierarchies have their root, their source, their being, and their existence. Perhaps the overshadowing World Soul sees to it that all religions and all faiths both past, present and future are the contact of the individual soul with the individual Oversoul, and the rapport of both with the Cosmic Oversoul.

Researching traditional religions of every culture points toward this purpose and meaning. That's why every religion is good for those souls involved within it and who find within it their pathway to God.

It must be remembered that to the initiates of the Mystery Schools, the various gods and goddesses of their philosophies and Schools were just as charged with meaning as the Christ or Buddha, or any of the other avatars are to many of us today, including Moses, overshadowed by Jehovah, the Father in heaven who "sent" him. And including any of the Ascended Masters of the Hindus, or Mohammed of the Muslims. The gods and goddesses of those ancient times directed the progression of the souls of their followers just as the Christ Spirit dominates the lives of Christian esotericists and mystics. The initiates and mystics of every faith today who still feel a cosmic contact with those ancient philosophers, gods and goddesses, still believe that Thoth, Osiris, Isis, Odin, Apollo, Hermes, Athena, Demeter or any of the other gods and goddesses can still be contacted today and their influence activated in a very definite manner.

The "Isis within" can be contacted and stimulated just as the "Christ within" is activated in the soul of the Western initiate. Most Christians — or those born into Christian orthodoxy — find that contacting the Isis within or the spirit of any deified force except that of Jesus, is unthinkable. Their inner perception encourages their belief that Christ is the only deified force aligned with their pathway of evolution. Thus they feel a natural disinclination to open the doorway of perception to any other force.

However, the true light seeker will find his/her perception not only open to all benefits of deity through Jesus and the Christ consciousness, but will opt to seek benefits and perception through the gods and goddesses of the past and the avatars of other great religions. It is easier for such an initiate to perceive a hierarchy of divine beings reaching from humans to the Godhead. It was best summarized by Iamblichus when writing of the gods and initiations of the Mystery Schools:

"Theurgy was magic, the last part of the sacerdotal science, and was practiced in the Greater Mysteries to evoke the appearance of superior beings. A theory upon which these Mysteries was based may be very briefly stated: There is ONE, prior to all beings, immovable, abiding in the solitude of His own unity. From THAT arises the supreme God, the Self-begotten, the good, the source of all things, the root, the god of gods, the First Cause, unfolding Himself into light. From Him springs the intelligible world or ideal universe. The universal mind, the Nous, and the incorporeal or intelligible gods belong to this. After this comes the World Soul to which belong the divine intellectual forms which are present with the visible bodies of the gods.

"Then come various hierarchies of superhuman beings — Archangels, Archons (rulers), or Cosmo-cratoras, Angels, Daimons, and so forth. Man is a being of a lower order, allied to these in his nature, and is capable of knowing them. This knowledge was achieved in the Mysteries and it led to union with God. In the Mysteries these doctrines are expounded — the progression from and the regression of all things to the One and the entire domination of the One. And further, these different beings were evoked and appeared, sometimes to teach, sometimes by their mere presence, to elevate and purify. The gods, being benevolent and propitious, impart their light to theurgists in unenvying abundance, calling upwards their souls to themselves, procuring them a union with themselves and accustoming them while they are yet in body to be separated from the body and to be led round to their eternal and intelligible principles.

"For the soul, having a twofold life — one being in conjunction with the body, the other being separate from all body — it is most necessary to learn to separate it from the body that thus it may unite itself with the gods by its intellectual and divine part, and learn the genuine principles of knowledge and the truths of the intelligible world. The presence of the gods indeed imparts to us the quality of the virtue of soul, purity of intellect and, in one word, elevates everything in us to its proper nature.

"It exhibits that which is not body as body to the eyes of the soul through those of the body. When the gods appear the soul receives liberation from the passions, a transcendent of perfection, and an energy entirely more excellent, and participates of divine love and an immense joy. By this we gain a divine life and are rendered in reality, divine. The culminating point of the Mysteries was when the initiate became a god, whether by union with a divine being outside himself, or by the realization of the divine self within him. This was termed ecstasy and was a state of what the Indian yogi would term high samadhi, the gross body being entranced and the freed soul perfecting its own union with the great One.

"This ecstasy is not a faculty properly so called. It is a state of the soul which transforms it in such a way that it then perceives what was previously hidden from it. The state will not be permanent until our union with God is irrevocable. Here in earth life, ecstasy is but a flash. Man can cease to become man and become god, but man cannot be god and man at the same time."

Plotinus declared that he had attained this ecstatic state three times in his life.

Religion and Philosophy

In the Mystery Schools the initiates recognized many godforces allied to the hierarchies. Each had its own place and function. Some of these gods and goddesses were creative agencies. Others performed the service of judgment. Others stimulated the spiritual and mental nature. Others were gods of compensation — some had a positive nature, others a negative. But all tended toward the ultimate purpose of lifting humankind out of material awareness and into the inevitable and celestial consciousness. "As above, so below — as in the great, so in the small."

Those who would become great must therefore associate with qualities of greatness in his/her spiritual and mental state. The initiates realized that in order for a godforce to manifest in their lives, they must place themselves in the position of receiving.

They believed that under the persuasion and assistance of the gods and goddesses, humankind could create its own world, dominating it and permitting its mental power to be drawn into a union with the powers of the hierarchy. They never substituted the lesser gods and goddesses with the One Great God. Rather, they accepted that each individual godforce was vivified and sustained by an influx of a still greater and invincible force.

QUESTION: Is it true that Jesus actually survived the crucifixion and returned to the Near East and India for many years until he died of old age?

ANSWER: I do not believe that Jesus actually "survived" the crucifixion. I do believe he went to Egypt, Greece and the Mystery Schools before his death during the years between twelve and thirty-three. I believe he was initiated into the Mysteries, which further enhanced his spiritual powers.

I also believe that before the Master came to Earth, he knew his primary mission was to so spiritualize his mortal body as to be beyond destruction, and his purpose was to demonstrate to all his future disciples that he could raise it again after it had been crucified, thus proving that his body was not subject to physical death as we know it. His resurrection also symbolized the truth of reincarnation. He was crucified on the cross, but he did not "die" on the cross, as we know death.

Perhaps he was actually in a state of suspended animation, if you will, until his body could be entombed, symbolizing the usual death. His spirit departed from his body, but the silver cord did not break, and while entombed, he was able to transmute the physical atoms of his body into etheric atoms and ascend into the higher planes of life. He is capable of appearing on any plane, the physical as well as any of the higher planes. So we of Earth could very well "see" him through a psychic or spiritual contact — if he so chooses.

QUESTION: Is the Shroud of Turin real or false as the Shroud of Jesus?

ANSWER: It's a matter of personal and individual opinion. The church has recently stated the cloth is not the Shroud of Jesus. But I choose to believe it is. They can't prove it isn't. I can't prove it is. But the process used in producing it was totally impossible, even in the 14th century. Each must consider what they see. The image there and all they can see in the Shroud is what makes it real to us. It's the image I believe in.

QUESTION: Does the cross have an esoteric and mystical meaning? — a hidden symbol?

ANSWER: One symbol of the cross represents man or woman (with the arms outstretched), and the human as the microcosm reflecting God the Macrocosm. Therefore, the cross is the symbol of God the masculine polarity, and Nature, the feminine polarity. The vertical portion of the cross turned downward represents the plant kingdom with its roots buried in the soil. Turned upward, it represents the human being (an inverted plant) receiving currents of spiritual ethers from celestial planes.

The horizontal arm represents the animal, which is between the plant and the human, and whose spine lies in a horizontal position to receive the currents of the animal group spirit which encircle the earth. Humans with their upright spines receive downpouring celestial ethers to be used in the evolution of the individualized soul.

The initiate Plato said, "The world-soul is crucified." By that, I believe he conveys the idea of the mystery of incarnation, the union of spirit and matter — Spirit inflowing into matter and giving it life, or God incarnating, descending the path of involution and (humanity) becoming spiritual, rising towards Godhood along the path of evolution.

The cross also symbolizes the phallus and the yoni, referring to the deep significance of the transmutation of the lower Self into the High Self. There was a time when humanity could generate from itself, plant-like, innocent, and inert. But when the spirit pierced the veil of flesh, and Adam knew his wife, he lost his inner perception and acquired outside, or objective consciousness.

The human race fell, but the same creative energy which

turned downward, when transmuted into love and spiritual energy, and finally turned upward, will be used for its rise and for its liberation. That is why the cross remains an emblem of everlasting life.

Chapter 2

Work of the Divine Hierarchy

QUESTION: What is the hierarchy?

ANSWER: The hierarchy is a group of great beings who are working together to help our metamorphosis into a higher life form. They work from the Buddhic level, which is the plane of love, reason and intuition.

How did the hierarchy come about? According to Theosophical teachings, nearly seventeen million years ago, a great being known as Sanat Kumara — the Ancient of Days, the Lord of the World — came from a higher world to take physical incarnation on this planet, to aid in the evolution of the Earth's lifewave of humanity. Due to the purity of Sanat's nature, and being a reflection of a far greater being — the Solar Logos — Sanat was only able to descend to the etheric level and assume an androgenous, etheric body.

Sanat's home is known as Shamballa, a city of light on one of Earth's etheric planes, located in the Gobi Desert. It would require a proficient, trained clairvoyant to see it since the entire city is composed of highest ethers.

With Sanat came the group of dedicated beings who formed themselves into what we call the hierarchy. They brought with them the energy of mind. This action by Sanat Kumara and the hierarchy speeded the evolution of humankind on this planet which would have required ages to develop. Since Atlantean time the hierarchy has remained hidden. Before that time they walked openly among humankind, but after the period of Atlantis they withdrew to manifest mainly from mental levels.

Through the ages, there have been Masters, teachers and angels of the hierarchy in each country, and in every spiritual tradition who were externalized, living in physical forms. On the whole, though, the hierarchy worked principally from higher levels through initiates and disciples. But now they are approaching closer to the Earth plane, merging more with Earth and human beings than at any other time. The hierarchy is planning to externalize more completely. This means that a great deal more, and a different kind of energy is coming into our planet and its ethers. This energy affects us on the mind (sentience) level.

If one's mind (sentience) is centered in the lower chakras below the solar plexus, this is where one will be stimulated. This is reflected in the many people who are interested only in materialism and other, lesser activities because their attention is centered there. But for those whose consciousness is centered on love and seeking the light — whose sentience is located in the higher chakras — a great opportunity opens for spiritual advancement and enlightenment.

Some of the beings of the hierarchy have already externalized and are living among us as disciples, as initiates, businessmen and women, as teachers, clergy, financiers, writers, creative workers, really in all walks of life. And many are already in position. But there are also those who are not yet "awakened." Many initiates — even members of the hierarchy — have not yet realized who they are. The Masters say that they came into birth as dedicated beings, but really don't know exactly how the mission they have fulfilled is going to help our destiny in the coming years.

The hierarchy needs workers now to assist humanities' great push into higher realms, especially with the current radical shifts in energy rays. Sixth Ray energy, that of devotion — the most active ray during the Piscean Age — is now becoming less active. The substance in our bodies and souls that responds to Sixth Ray energy is being replaced. This new matter, which responds to the Aquarian Age energies of love and wisdom, is being stimulated through the higher chakras. Thus a change is coming. The hierarchy knows that only those souls responding to love and wisdom energies will be moving forward with the lifewave entering the Aquarian Age.

I am a disciple of the Master Kuthumi, who is a part of the inner hierarchy. His purpose is to work through various Earth sensitives to bring about teachings which open the way for New Age perceptions to penetrate the consciousness of light seekers as the lifewave moves into the ethers of Aquarius. There are special Orders in existence composing the divine hierarchy. One of these Orders is that called the order of Melchizedek — Melchizedek being a representative of Sanat Kumara, the God of our lifewave on this planet. Kuthumi is linked to the order of Melchizedek. Melchizedek is one of the manifestations of Sanat.

Melchizedek has been mentioned in the Bible, the first reference being in Genesis 14:18. Abraham and Lot were separated because of Lot's capture by their enemies. They were celebrating Lot's return "and Melchizedek, King of Salem, brought forth bread and wine; and he was the priest of the Most High God." The second reference is in Psalms 110:4, which reads "the Lord hath sworn, and will not repent, Thou art a priest for ever after the order of Melchizedek." The next reference is in the New Testament in Paul's letter to the Hebrews, 5:6, "As he saith also in another place, Thou are a priest for ever after the order of Melchizedek" — and 5:10, to establish the authority of Jesus to the Hebrews, Paul said, "called of God a high priest after the order of Melchizedek." In 6:20, he said, "whither the forerunner is for us entered, even Jesus, made a high priest for ever after the order of Melchizedek." In 7:1, "For this Melchizedek, king of Salem, priest of the most high God, who met Abraham..and blessed him." Further references are in Verses 10-11 and in Verses 15 through 17.

Sanat Kumara is our Planetary Logos, guiding this planet under the direction of the Solar Logos, who is the trinity of the Father, Son and Holy Spirit (Mother). This planet is linked to a solar hierarchy, reaching far beyond this planet, its solar system and this galaxy. One of the major centers of this hierarchy is on the planet Sirius, where the order of Melchizedek has its foundation. (Sirius is a star in the constellation Canis Major, meaning "big dog." It is in the Southern Hemisphere, approximately 8.7 light years from Earth. It is the brightest star in the Southern Hemisphere.)

Now comes a question of initiation with which we are all consumed these days. These Earth initiations are simply forward steps as we ourselves attempt to become integrated into the divine hierarchy.

Earth itself is now facing its own initiation into the Aquarian Age. This perhaps points to the reason we are experiencing some of the tribulations many teachers have been prophesying between now and the year 2100. Earth simply will purify herself in order to experience the cosmic initiation properly and assume her place as a link in the Cosmic Hierarchy — not the human hierarchy, but the Cosmic Hierarchy. And she will purify herself because she will enter the main stream of Cosmic

Evolution. In so doing we may find it difficult to measure up to her need to purify her streams and ethers which we have contaminated. But purify them she will, someway, somehow.

The Master Jesus came to Earth at the beginning of the Piscean Age and gave himself to the cross so that he might focus the White Light of the Christ to diminish the cloud of karma which had surrounded the Earth plane at that time. His crucifixion did just that. It was called the "remission of sins for humanity." His blood sacrifice wiped away that karmic cloud so far as the Piscean Age was concerned. We have again created a negative karmic situation. Will the Christ come again to submit to something similar to a crucifixion to again demolish our karma? No.

It rests with us to clear away our own karma and if we do not, Mother Nature herself — the Earth Mother — will simply take it upon herself to do it. But the karma must be leveled away before this little planet, this great Mother of ours, can enter the Age of Aquarius purified. Initiates and disciples of the hierarchy must send forth the white light, because the white light is sufficient to demolish the darkness of world karma, and to erase fear. This purification will require the efforts of all human beings in distributing the white light to overcome the darkness of the karma which has accumulated around the planet.

Many souls of this lifewave will face the "judgment day" of the great cosmic evolution. This simply means they will be reborn on a planet which is somewhere coming into a Piscean Age expression. And the light seekers shall proceed into the Aquarian Age either on this planet or on another more evolved.

QUESTION: What is the hierarchical plan into which we all must fit?

ANSWER: Our hierarchy constitutes that group of spiritual beings on the inner planes of our solar system who control the evolutionary processes of Earth's human lifewave.

The God of our solar system, the Solar Logos, is a trinity — the Father, the Son and the Holy Spirit, or will, love-wisdom and active intelligence. This Trinity in unity reflects as three Rays of Aspect and four Rays of Attribute:

1. Will or power;
2. Love-wisdom;
3. Active intelligence;
4. Harmony-Beauty;
5. Concrete knowledge;
6. Devotion-Idealism and
7. Ceremonial magic.

These are what Ancient Wisdom call the Seven Rays present now in our ethers.

The Sixth Ray — that of devotion-idealism — has dominated the consciousness of people during the Piscean Age which is now closing. The dominant Ray of the Aquarian Age will be that of love-wisdom — that is, after our lifewave is separated.

The planetary hierarchy is a reflection of our solar hierarchy. Sanat Kumara is the Lord of the World. Under this Lord are the twelve Kumaras (Buddhas of Activity). Three of these esoteric Kumaras work with Sanat Kumara and the Buddhas of Activity to complete seven Planetary Manifestations.

There are four other cosmic beings whose work is:

1. Adjustment of karma;
2. Keeping of Akashic Records;
3. Participants in solar councils; and
4. Guiding human evolution.

The remaining personnel of the hierarchy are divided into three main and four subsidiary groups, each of which is being presided over by one of those whom we call the three Great Lords — the Manu, the Boddhisattva and the Mahachohan.

The Manu, head of the first subsidiary group, manipulates matter and is occupied in the evolution of forms. The Manu's work is with governments, races and planetary politics. To him is committed the will and purpose of the Planetary Logos. The Manu is the focal point of will.

The Boddhisattva, the World Teacher, is the head of the second group and is the focal point of the love-wisdom aspect of the Logos. He is the great Lord of Love and Compassion. Through him flows the energy of the second aspect, reaching him directly from the heart center of the Planetary Logos via the heart of Sanat Kumara. The World Teacher is occupied with evolving life within the form. His work is with religions and faiths.

The Mahachohan, or the Lord of Civilization, is the head of the third group. He is the sum total of the intelligence aspect and deals with spirit and matter, strengthening the relation between them. He manipulates the forces of nature and is largely the emanating source of electrical energy. His work is through science, education and civilization.

The work of the hierarchy is to raise the consciousness of humanity by these three departments until each soul can mount to the Logos and find union with the Self of the solar system. Each soul can raise his or her consciousness no matter which of these three lines of approach one chooses. We can reach goals via the path of the Manu, the World Teacher or the Lord of Civilization. But note that on this planet the Lord of Love and Power in the first Kumara is the focal point for all three departments. He is the one Initiator and whether one works in line of power, in line of love or of intelligence, one must finally find one's goal on the attribute ray of love and wisdom.

Love was the source, love is the goal, and love the method of attainment.

This is the hierarchical plan into which we all must fit. We must all become aware of our origin—how and why we came down into matter and are finding our way toward our origin, toward the Solar Logos. It is essential that we learn the plan of the hierarchy and make conscious efforts to aid that plan. This plan is evolution, liberation of the ego from matter after full Self-consciousness is attained and each soul becomes a law unto itself.

Since New Age Mystery Schools are connected closely with the hierarchy, it is the purpose of their Teachers to do all in their power to help each disciple attain that goal during his or her present incarnation.

QUESTION: If the hierarchy guides us through a subjective government, how does their governmental structure relate to our democratic form of government?

ANSWER: If we accept the Hermetic axiom, "As above so below," then our democratic government must reflect that of the planetary hierarchy and consequently conform to the cosmic law of evolution.

Even in ancient days when tribes formed Earth's population, they chose a leader who was expected to organize sources for food and protection. Later there were kings and queens who reigned over their subjects. Since before written history, a central authority has always been established. This authority assumed different forms. A king governed as a monarchy, a government by one. Priests formed a governmental hierarchy. Oligarchy constituted government by a few — nobility or a caste. Then there came despotism or government by tyranny.

As individuals gradually became aware of their own inner powers, they began to rebel against dictators and tyrannical despots, especially when they were self-proclaimed. With the spread of Christianity 2,000 years ago, the race began a struggle for freedom. "The Kingdom of God is within you" taught Jesus, causing the populace to doubt the power of kings. "Love ye one another." "Do good to those who hate you." Such teachings of self-empowerment cost him his life. During the early days of Christianity, the Church became the principal government, imposing the Inquisition upon the people, alternating power with presiding kings.

As populations increased, monarchs discovered it was no longer possible to impose taxes upon people without their being represented in government. Countries were divided into districts, states, or provinces with each represented in a parliamentary government and kings shared their power with their subjects. Even so, as the populations demanded more and more freedom, revolution after revolution followed and gave rise to Constitutional Governments. This gave rise to social and democratic movements in the world.

Eventually labor parties were organized. Women organized and demanded equal opportunity and freedom. With the ending of the first World War, many monarchies and kingdoms were relics of history. As the movement of the world progress is spiral or cyclic, and every action has its reaction, we are alternating between nationalism and ideas of a one world government.

But regardless, we know that democracy is here to stay. With the fall of communism in Russia, and its decline in popularity in China, most of the world is embracing forms of democracy. When the reaction to the fall of communism is over, and the wheels of time turn again, another major movement will be made toward more freedom. Then governments, no matter what their form, will be shaped by people who will serve the people.

With the New Age seekers of light expanding, these governments will be formed by men and women who are familiar with the plans of the divine hierarchy and anxious to pattern world governments after and with spiritual foundations — men and women who know their Higher Selves and the unity of all Selves — women and men of vision who are one in heart and one in will. When this time comes, the only governments needed will be those who plan ways to spread more light and love. "As above, so below" will have become a reality.

QUESTION: What can we do to develop our own conscious awareness of the hierarchy and discover how we can best be of service as the New Age evolves?

ANSWER: We can develop our own conscious awareness voluntarily and deliberately by purifying our physical, emotional and mental bodies. Purity is from within outward. Asceticism may be strictly applied without spiritual results if it begins from the wrong side. It could focus the attention unduly on physical things, resulting in austerity, not the quality of purity needed for conscious awareness.

But when it is the result of true discernment and an awareness of spiritual values, purity reveals an inner development rather than a mere self-disciplinary act of personal will. We can purify our physical bodies by clean and hygienic living; we can and should pay strict attention to our diets, avoiding such foods as meat, alcoholic and other harmful beverages, avoiding tobacco, drugs and all the harmful habits which burden our systems with poisonous substances. It is essential to have healthy bodies to offer the Masters and angels of the hierarchy as effective channels for our Higher Selves to express — we must be very sure the purity is for the enhancement of our souls, and not simply to display an exemplary body and its beauty to the world for the sake of vanity.

We can purify our astral bodies by positively expressing and then releasing difficult emotions such as fear, jealousy, hatred, anger, greed and transmuting such passions and worldly desires into spiritual seeking — by following the dictates of our consciences and keeping our thoughts constantly attuned to our Higher Selves. Meditation or prayer is a sure method for such attunement.

Meditation trains the mind toward one-pointedness. Gradually — sheath by sheath — we unveil the High Self until we consciously respond to its higher vibrations and its glory is revealed. Meditation leads us to the realization that we are children of God. Alignment with our Oversouls allows the spiritual forces to be poured into us and awaken in us new and higher levels of consciousness. Through prayer we can listen to the Voice of Silence and awaken our intuition.

After we have developed conscious awareness to the vibrations of the Oversoul, we can aid the development of consciousness in our immediate environment — by living the principles of truth, by our example, by radiating love and light, by creating such a magnetic field that those around us will be influenced by it. And by inspiring and supporting one another, we will all try to lead pure lives.

The principles begin with self-respect and love, constant unselfish service, by spreading the ageless Wisdom, by sharing a New Age vision, by inspiring others to a new life and awakening in them a new consciousness, the consciousness of their own Higher Selves. Thus they may develop their consciousness and become co-workers in the hierarchical plan of service. This inspiring of others must be accomplished by working on ourselves and remaining open to learning from all around us. Avoiding feelings of superiority and refraining from telling others what is best for them is essential.

QUESTION: What Earth activities would you consider being representative of the work of the divine hierarchy?

ANSWER: All movements with philanthropic or altruistic purposes, particularly the educational and religious movements. To name particular movements would be a personal opinion, as it is not possible to verify the statements made directly. However, I would consider the following movements as such.

In the governmental or political scene, the present day democratic movements as they should be operating. The Bolshevistic movement — the great experiment for socialism and communism in Russia — may have been part of the Great Plan to demonstrate how materialistic communism cannot succeed. The Feminist and Civil Rights Movements show progress and advancement toward freedom and equality.

In the field of education — specifically the explosion in physical fitness and wellbeing, the move toward better diets and physical purification — have certainly accomplished a great deal. They prove that people are becoming aware there is physical law as well as mental and spiritual laws and the violation of Nature's law will result in disease. Certainly we know that medicines often suppress the symptoms and do not remove the causes of diseases. Coming to the fore in the New

Age are the movements of osteopathy, chiropractic, naprapathy (connective tissue doctrine of disease), neuropathy, the anti-vaccination, the anti-vivisection activities. And the vegetarian movement is spreading beyond belief. Also, mental and metaphysical healing, practical psychology, family therapy, biofeedback, etc.

In the field of religion and philosophy, the following movements may be considered as being advanced by the Masters: Eastern yoga and meditation activities, Unitarianism, Spiritualism, Native American Indian Spirituality, Liberal Catholicism, liberal theology in Judaism, Christian Science, New Thought, Theosophy, Mysticism, Ancient Wisdom teachings involving Self-realization, the return of the Mystery Schools. All these movements reveal different phases of truth and appeal to different individuals according to their capacity and spiritual unfoldment.

Theosophy, Mysticism and Ancient Wisdom are quite important movements, as they definitely reveal the plan of the hierarchy and seek the conscious cooperation of humans to further that plan. They appeal only to a comparative few who are willing to study these teachings and apply them to their lives.

The New Thought movement is similar to the Theosophic movement, but it appeals to many because great emphasis is laid by their leaders on physical health and material prosperity. Christian Science is similar to New Thought, but it is almost entirely a healing movement. The remaining movements are mostly religious organizations.

Mention also should be made of the great "secret society" and lodge movements of the world, more particularly the Masons, who have unspoken esoteric purposes. And the order of the Eastern Star, whose object has been to further the work of preparing for the coming World Teacher.

QUESTION: How can we best apply the knowledge of the divine hierarchy and the gods of the Mystery Schools toward our own Self-realization and enlightenment in the Aquarian Age?

ANSWER: Initiates and mystics of today cannot help but have felt a stirring within, a reaching back to initiations in the ancient past, a stirring of age-old memories. Yet strive as we will, most of us cannot fully awaken the being that we were. Thus we subconsciously turn toward symbology and a ceaseless struggle to interpret symbols as they were presented in the ancient Mysteries. We may not be able to recreate the formal rituals of our previous initiations, but we constantly subconsciously recognize symbols as the language of eternal truths. We reach for intuitive knowledge through the language of symbology.

For instance, the sun — we strive constantly to recognize its symbolic form. We realize its chief significance is of the Logos — that it is also connected with the star Logoi; with the Ancient Egyptians, with the symbol of Krishna, the Buddha, the Christ, and other avatars. We realize, too, that this particular symbol touches in some way all those whose lives conform with the general tenor of Logoidal consciousness.

To see or study particular symbols starts a chain reaction of ideas, teachings and learnings once received under the guidance of a hierophant or under the inspiration of the inner planes. We struggle for, but are not usually truly aware of the gradual development of consciousness into a permanent illumination. Slowly comes the realization that once we were taught that even the physical form was a symbol, a visible proof of divine archetypes.

There is a very real basis for the axiom, "One picture is

worth a thousand words," but often we need to be reminded that consciously or unconsciously one is influenced by the shape, arrangement, color and form of the symbols around them.

In the Masonic Lodge, for instance, the scintillating letter G shines over the throne of the Worshipful Master "in the East." We can accept the symbol as representing "God" or "Geometry" or even "God Geometrizes." Such a striking symbol brings the consciousness of all the brothers of the lodge into unity. They cannot help but focus upon the meaning of the symbol and the awakening of innate wisdom through it. Although we, as initiates, cannot "picture" a cosmic force, we can easily picture a god or goddess who has become a symbol of that force. The Masons even now wear aprons upon which symbols indicate the status of their degree standing.

We know without question that the hierarchy — including the order of Melchizedek — consists of numerous divine powers or forces. And we know that the early gods and goddesses took upon themselves the task of representing various types of divine power. We know too that with the departure of the gods and goddesses from Earth, the divine force they represented eventually came to be called simply the manifestations of divine power. Since the gods and goddesses of the hierarchy are our ancestors, those of us who recognize them as such can only accept now the symbols which represent them.

When they ruled over initiation and the Mysteries in those long ago days they allowed themselves to become symbolized. For they knew quite well of the millennium between their manifestation on Earth, their disappearance from Earth, and the time of their return. They knew too that the nature of humankind would relegate them to the level of symbology. But they realized that those of us who have the will to know and receive illumination recognize that our efforts at coming into rapport with them and the supernal Godhead depended on our own unfolding consciousness. Our own consciousness must be the magnet that attracts the descending universal power and force.

In those faraway days, we as initiates realized there was an all enfolding, all encompassing power constantly seeking to express itself in form. Now, however, forgetful of the Mysteries and our own initiations, we seem to have adopted the attitude that we are supreme. We seldom open our consciousness to realize there are beings more highly evolved than we are. We feel that the cosmic force should operate in our behalf. The gods and hierophants of the Mystery Schools realize that the infinitesimal mind of humankind could only grasp the greatness of the celestial force by dividing it into several aspects. In H. G. Wells' Outline of History, we find these inspired remarks:

"When we direct our attention to those new accumulations of human beings that were beginning in Egypt and Mesopotamia, we find that one of the most conspicuous and constant objects in all these cities is a temple or a group of temples. In some cases there arises beside it, in these regions, a royal palace. But as often as not the temple towered over the palace. All over the ancient civilized world we find them. Wherever primitive civilization has set its foot — in Africa, Europe, or Western Asia — a temple arose. And where the civilization is most ancient — in Egypt and in Sumer — there the temple is most in evidence.

"The beginnings of civilization and the appearance of temples is simultaneous in history. The two belong together. The beginning of cities is the temple stage of history. The earliest civilized governments were essentially priestly governments. It was not kings and captains who first set men to the plow and a settled life. It was the ideas of the gods, working with the acquiescence of common men. The early rulers of Sumer we know were all priests-kings only because they were chief priests."

With the coming of the gods and the establishment of the Mystery Schools, the initiate realized s/he possessed a soul — and even more, that there existed a divine Oversoul of which s/he was a reflection. The initiates knew too, of the World Soul that exists beyond the material plane. They not only realized there was a system by which this World Soul could be contacted — it was indeed this system with which they could come in contact after their initiation. Every initiate realized that the superconscious mind was always in rapport with the World Soul, even though s/he might not be consciously aware of its existence. The initiate learned how to permit the superconscious mind to dominate his/her consciousness, thus coming into attunement with its supernal vibrations.

But the uninitiated camouflage their natural reactions. So narrowed have their perceptions become that it is necessary for them to enter into special practices to awaken the inner intuitive consciousness again. There are ways a consciousness may be drawn into closer harmony with the World Soul. The World Soul is the domain of nature gods and divine powers. Coming in touch with the World Soul is coming into contact with the nature forces, the elements, the divine powers, and working consciously with them for the benefit of both.

QUESTION: Please tell more of Sanat Kumara.

ANSWER: The order of Melchizedek has impressed upon many spiritual seekers that the time is now at hand for establishing continuous instruction in the Ancient Wisdom. This being true, it is important to discuss Sanat Kumara.

Stories tell us that Sanat Kumara came to Earth from a much higher etheric plane on Venus some sixteen and one-half million years ago. How they came, this Sanat Kumara and companions, we are not told, but that it was via a physical transportation we are certain. Interplanetary traveling, you must know, is possible and will some day be an established fact. These beings brought with them the food which is known among us as "wheat." This is why we deduced that physical transportation was involved.

Sanat Kumara in certain of the sacred books is called the "Eternal Virgin-Youth." "Kumara" means ruler. Ageless, and presenting an ethereal image of astonishing beauty, being ever youthful in appearance, Sanat is androgenous — being neither masculine nor feminine. In build s/he is more handsomely perfect than Apollo/Aphrodite, whose facial features Sanat Kumara's somewhat resemble. It is believed in mystical schools that the sculptor who fashioned the famous Apollo, or the immortal Venus had seen Sanat Kumara, and actually sought to immortalize the vision that was his for one brief visit to the Sacred Land.

Sanat Kumara's etheric skin is creamy in color, seemingly smooth like chiffon-velvet in its texture, and radiant with an inherent luster that makes Sanat appear unwordly. In the dark, Sanat Kumara glows like a soft light. The eyes are sometimes lambent pools of light, peacock-blue in coloring — flickering with a spectrum of life. The hair, divided in the center of the head, falls in heavy waves to the shoulders and is like burnished gold. One perceives Sanat to be continuously crowned with a halo of white light — as Tennyson would say, "Mystic, wonderful." The extended right hand is a scepter, and from it flows a stream of Fohat — cosmic electricity — that is available for humankind's benefit. Sanat absorbs physical sustenance from the atmosphere, just as the human race will do in the Seventh Major period; and elimination, following assimilation, is through a process of exudation and odorless evaporation.

In motion, Sanat seems to float rather than walk; and every movement is productive of a gently spiritual music.

Sanat Kumara and the other beings arrived upon our world during the Fourth Round, and in the middle of the Lemurian cycle, just after the separation of the sexes. The purpose of their coming was threefold:

I. To quicken the mental evolution of humanity;
II. To found the Mystery Schools upon Earth; and
III. To assume the hierarchical government of the world.

Twelve of these came to the Earth with Sanat Kumara; six of them still tarry with us. The others, their work finished, entered into higher planes of evolution. Of Sanat Kumara and the six Kumaras who remain, it is written:

> Four sacrificed themselves
> For the sins of the world
> And for the instruction of the ignorant.
>
> Oh, Disciple, thou shalt never speak
> Of these great ones before the world,
> Mentioning them by name.
> The wise alone will understand.
> — The Upanishads

Sanat Kumara wears the same ethereal body as was worn upon Venus; the other beings also came "across" in ethereal form. They did not take incarnation in our physical humanity, but by materialization created for themselves bodies which are the archetypes of our perfected humanity. They have worn these bodies from that day to this.

Many of the Venusians incarnated into our terrestrial humanity, conceived children with them, and so helped to evolve Earth humans to the point where they could and did receive "the spark of mind." These beings, moving among humanity, shone upon it as spiritual suns upon spiritual flowers, drawing their lower selves upwards, thus quickening the germs of mental life so that they burst into growth and thought was born.

I suggest you give some portion of your daily meditation to a visualization of Sanat Kumara, for, in a sense, Sanat embodies the physical ideal for initiates who are the consecrated progenitors of the coming new lifewave.

Chapter 3

The Wisdom Teachings in Sacred Texts

QUESTION: What did Jesus mean when he said, "I will give you eternal life" and "Let the dead bury their dead?"

ANSWER: The Earth plane is certainly not the plane of eternal life. Earth is the plane of opposites — life and death, light and darkness, day and night, good and evil. So he had to have been referring to life on the spirit side. When he said, "I will give you eternal life," he also said something else. Remember when he was speaking to a certain disciple who wanted Jesus and his disciples to pause long enough to bury a dead relative? He said, "Let the dead bury their dead." What could Jesus have meant by that? Initiates both on Earth and in heaven consider Earth to be the plane of "the dead," because human beings are not awakened. We are "dead" in a spiritual sense. We have not yet arrived at the epitome of awakening. Some of us have broken through the shell. We are entering the dawning of our awakening, but when we actually come into our spiritual awakening we will understand what a tremendous difference there is between our present consciousness and our consciousness then.

So when he said, "Let the dead bury their dead," he meant to let the unawakened ones bury the dead relative because these people are spiritually dead. In other words, human beings are the walking dead to the high initiates because they have not yet come into a state of total enlightenment. He did not mean anything derogatory — he simply meant people are still in a state of a waking trance that has not yet come into full Self-realization.

Now when he said, "I will give you eternal life," he was promising to take you into the spheres of immortality Overthere after your death. That's eternal life. He was promising: "I will take you through the astral plane, through the mental plane, even through the lower causal plane, into the plane of immortality." That's the plane of eternal life. The lower planes are the planes from which we come and go — we reincarnate and reincarnate back and forth — until we have gained Self-realization. Then when we die we pass over into the high causal plane. That's the plane of immortality.

When all the karma, all the desires that pull the soul back down to rebirth are vanquished and overcome, the soul enters the high causal at the time of death and need not ever reincarnate again, but can dwell eternally in the spirit world and continue evolving Overthere. "Overcome" is the word he used. He was promising to give you eternal life by taking you to dwell in the plane of immortality. You need "go out no more from the Father's House." That will be your eternal home. The only way we can go from there is to higher celestial spheres. We won't come back to Earth again.

QUESTION: Please explain what Jesus meant when he said "I and my Father are one."

ANSWER: We have all arrived at a point of understanding wherein we realize that ignorance of the law excuses no one from its natural consequence. We perceive also that we are punished by our sins, and not for them, as so many people believe.

Understanding this law of Cause and Effect, or Action and Reaction, still in our human weakness we too often are deceived by outer appearance. We fail to judge as Jesus taught us to, with righteous judgment, and so we allow ourselves to become the victims of negative beliefs, depressions and other forms of fear; when by simply stopping to quietly realize the God or the Good within us, and our oneness with it, we might have true peace of mind, wholeness of body and beauty of circumstance.

In other words we must KNOW that we were created by Divine Mind operating through law upon it's own substance which is perfection, peace, wholeness, beauty and love. Thus, the real you and I must necessarily reflect the qualities of our source, and already possess within us those attributes.

Let's go a bit deeper into this thought, and see just WHY these things are true — which is "In the beginning, God ..." By this phrase we mean the beginning of any created thing — anything which has visible form. For instance, we might use the illustration of a farmer sowing his grain. In the beginning here means before his crop is created by the laws of Nature. Each thing of form must have a beginning and an end. Each good or evil circumstance must have a beginning, each of life's many experiences have a beginning. We might say of this thought in relationship to the physical body, "in the beginning" before illness or deformity appeared, or before any form of inharmony began to manifest upon either the mental, spiritual or physical planes of being.

Eternal spirit is always and forever perfect. It knows no other law than the perfect law of its source, the Infinite Creator.

Certainly we cannot suppose any beginning to the Infinite Creator, whom we shall designate as Absolute (All) Intelligence and Absolute First Cause. There never was a time when God began to be, or when He/She was not. So "In the beginning, God was." Nothing existed other than God, whose attributes are Absolute (All) Intelligence, Limitless Imagination, Perfect Consciousness and complete Self-Expression. This God with infinite potentialities filled all space.

The Bible's story of creation says that "The spirit of God moved ..." Then it follows that it could only move upon Itself, for it, (Infinite Intelligence — God) filled all space, and there was nothing outside of Itself. All movement then is an interior movement of the great Life Principle (God) upon Itself, (Primal Substance).

It follows then, that all ideas, or the creative mental patterns for all forms already existed in the limitless Mind of God before the Universal Law, impelled by Infinite Intelligence (Divine mind — Spirit) moves to create. This inner movement of the spirit upon itself we shall call Self-contemplation. This term denotes an inner awareness, an awareness that must be complete and perfect. Therefore God's expression, or the manifold things created by God, must always be harmonious and perfect, because their source — God — is Harmony and Perfection.

Jesus expressed the true relationship of human beings with God when He said, "The Father and I are one." We shall discover as we seek further that the creative spirit of God works in and through each of us and that the power which we seek, we already possess in fullness.

Jesus said further that the very words which He spoke were creative, for they were spirit and they were life. Every time we think or speak we use, as he did, the creative energy of God.

Because of immutable Law our thought and speech creates exactly according to the quality of our thinking and speaking. Thoughts and speech are more than things; they are the creative CAUSE of things. Mentally and spiritually we were created in the image and likeness of God. Thus our thought energy is God power flowing through us into expression. The Bible says, "You must let the mind be in you that was in Christ Jesus." This means the perfect Mind of God, for God can only work for us by working through us. In other words, we are the instrument through which God expresses divine will for us, which is always perfection and all good.

To be able to use this creative power wisely and constructively is the real wisdom which we are each seeking. Knowledge alone can guarantee freedom from bondage to ignorance and error. Self-recognition alone, or the realization that we are one with the Creator and His powers and perfection, can produce that knowledge. Thus we see WHY Jesus also said, "Ye shall know the truth, and the truth shall make ye free." Free from all inharmonies and limitations. Free to express outwardly the perfection and glory of the perfect inner spirit, which is of God.

QUESTION: Is the consecration of bread and wine into the body and blood of Jesus, as explained in the Bible, a Roman "pagan" rite introduced by the church fathers and does transmutation really take place?

ANSWER: The answer to the first part of your question is, no, it was not introduced by the church fathers. The rite of Holy Communion dates back to the days of antiquity in the temples of the Mysteries, long preceding even those of Egypt.

But I'm sure there have been changes made since then in the ceremony used today by the Christian churches, because the ceremony in the Mysteries had a deep physical and mystical implication, totally esoteric — while that of today is mostly exoteric.

The symbolic use of the bread and juice of the grape remains much the same. In the days of antiquity the hierophant — through powerful, esoteric processes and ceremonies — endowed the wine and bread with his or her own powers. Through alchemical processes, one could draw the Divine Substance from the ethers through and impart it to the bread and wine. In the days of antiquity, the partaking of the wine and bread was only for the disciple who was prepared for initiation. It was a part of their initiation ceremony.

The orthodox Christian church of today truly believes in the potency of the Sacrament. They believe that the rite of Holy Communion or Eucharist does, in some mysterious way, imbue the sincere seeker with a minute portion of the actual body and blood of Christ — while we mystics believe it imbues the seeker with the great body of light the Lord Jesus manifested on the Mount of Transfiguration.

When he said, "This is my body and this is my blood," I know that mystics believe he referred to his Body of Light. It is that mystical Body and that mystical Blood of which we partake. We believe we take into our own bodies some small measure of Everlasting Life when we partake of his divine Body of Light and we gain a small measure of soul salvation or liberation from rebirth. We do not think of his physical form and physical blood — but of the Body of his Divinity. We feel that by doing so we are united more closely to his Divine Heart and are made more worthy to be called a true child of light.

QUESTION: How do the once secret teachings of the Bhagavad Gita compare with those of modern Mystery Schools so far as the Oversoul (High Self) is concerned?

ANSWER: The Gita speaks of the High Self as the Supreme Spirit. The Gita says that when the spirit departs from the body at death it "goes forth taking the powers with Him as the wind carries perfumes with it. Through learning, seeing, touch, taste and smell, He partakes of the objects of sense."

The Gita calls "the Supreme Spirit" the "beholder" of all the varied manifestations of its forms. The Supreme Spirit — the Oversoul — is the "thinker," who expresses itself through the mind, as a musician makes his or her musical instruments express him/herself. The Spirit is the "upholder," the defender of the forms, the one who vitalizes the forms and supplies the energy for their evolution. It is the "taster," one who registers the sensations and communicates with the external world through the sense organs. It is the Supreme Spirit, therefore the "Lord, the Highest Self."

When the Supreme Spirit incarnates, it gathers all the knowledge and experience it can, and when it departs the body, it takes away with it the experience and the powers it gathered, as a musician retains the ability to plan and express that talent after the musical instrument is laid down, or even after it is broken to pieces.

Modern Mystery Schools also teach that the Supreme Spirit merges with matter and form through hearing, seeing, touch, taste and smell — all the sense organs. It makes itself one with, and vibrates in each atomic life, and after it has learned all there is to be learned, it aligns all the three vehicles within the causal periphery and stabilizes them therein, thus accomplishing the work for which it was incarnated.

So it seems that insofar as the Supreme Spirit is concerned, these teachings parallel each other.

QUESTION: Please explain "The Word" as it appears in Biblical writings.

ANSWER: The Logos has come to mean a great being who stands between humanity and God. The Logos is sometimes called The Word. According to the Gospel of St. John, the Logos is the great being, the God, from whom Jesus came. Several verses point to the fact that Jesus was the son of this God (Chapter 1): "In the beginning was the Word and the Word was with God, and the Word was God. The same was in the beginning with God. All things were made by Him and without Him was not anything made that was made. In Him was life; and the life was the light of men. And the light shineth in the darkness; and the darkness comprehend it not. There was a man sent from God, whose name was John."

Now here we have John describing the Word which was God, and the Word which was with God. Thus we have God the Logos, or the Father; and Christ the Logos, the Son who was with God in the beginning. It was this Logos God who was the Creator of our particular solar system, and Christ His Son was with him from the beginning.

Now this God, the Creator of the solar system, sent forth John, or spoke to John, and told him that he must begin baptizing by water, but there would come another, His Son, who would be the Light of the World, and who would baptize with fire. And the sign John was to look for was the dove descending like a spirit to sit upon His Son. Therefore, when John saw Jesus coming toward him to be baptized and he saw the spiritual

The Wisdom Teachings in Sacred Texts 63

symbol descending to sit upon Jesus, he said: "This is the one that God told me He was sending. Therefore, I can bear witness that this man is the Son of God — the Light of the World."

And the voice of the Father Logos spoke and said: "Thou art my beloved son in whom I am well pleased." Thus the first Logos becomes the Father Logos and the second Logos becomes the Christ. And it is He who overshadowed Jesus. It was He that Jesus called his "Father in heaven." It was this planetary god — this Christos, the Logos Creator of our planet — who was with God in the beginning. It was He who spoke to John and told him that another would come forward who would be the light of the world, and he was to recognize this one by the sign of the dove descending to sit upon him.

This Logos Word who was with God in the beginning, and who is the planetary god of our Earth, has descended to become the celestial double of all the great lights through the past ages. That is why Abraham, Moses, Krishna, Buddha, Osiris, Jesus, Mohammed, Mother Mary, Isis and other great teachers and avatars have appeared upon Earth as children of God. To the Jew, the Hindu, the Buddhist, the Moslem, their great avatar also came as the child of God and "the Light of the World." This is true for all of them, and all are teachers of the highest order and children of God.

Chapter 4

Death and the Soul

QUESTION: Would you please address the subject of suicide as it relates to the soul? What about physicians and their assistance in helping the terminally ill die with dignity?

ANSWER: In addressing the subject of suicide as it relates to the soul, it will vary with the individual. One can say on Earth, "If a robbery is committed of ten thousand dollars, you are incarcerated for ten years. But if it is a hundred thousand dollars, it is for many more years." That is easy when the human race makes laws. But when dealing with karmic law, one cannot define the regulations so easily, nor assign specific punishments to specific wrongdoing.

Karma may manifest in innumerable ways. It may be divided into a thousand different moments or incidents in time. The soul of the person who has committed suicide may be held on the astral near Earth after death, doing service for those left behind — to whom they would have given service — until the time arrives when the soul would have passed over through a natural death. Or, it may be that in another rebirth that soul will be given an opportunity of performing greater service to those it abandoned.

It is certainly not true that suicides are always relegated to the planes of punishment. How could they then work out their debts of service? No, a soul is always placed where it can solve its problems best. If its problems seem insurmountable during any one incarnation, in some coming life that soul will be placed among those same problems again so that it will, at some time on its evolutionary pathway, learn how to work through those particular circumstances.

There is no way of escaping the effect of the law of karma. You may have problems that you feel are greater than you can bear. You may think that through suicide you escape them. But you do not, for these problems you have created are ingrained in your permanent seed atoms and destiny pattern until you change the atoms. Modifying the atoms through a transformation of consciousness, by acquiring spiritual-emotional qualities and through purification of the physical temple — these things alone constitute escape from self-made destiny.

The soul who commits suicide is not denied the opportunity of working out whatever debts it may owe. Nor is it denied any good karma it may have earned. There is no soul so bad it does not have some good karma in its incarnation. Nor is there one so good that it does not have some ill here and there. The "unbearable" problems must some day be faced and overcome, whether as service to others from the higher planes, or in a future life.

Now, as for physicians giving assistance to the terminally ill, this is a matter to be discussed between each patient and his or her doctor. It must be remembered that we are speaking of physicians aiding only those patients who are terminal, with no hope of recovery, and who are in agony. If they are being kept alive by medical methods which only prolong their suffering and death, then this is interfering with and prolonging the natural time of their death.

Some doctors believe that it is their duty to prolong life as much as possible regardless how much the poor patient is suffering. They consider it to be an achievement to use any method to keep patients alive — often long past the time of natural death. Some believe that physicians who aid in dying are interfering with the will of God by releasing these souls sooner than God's will. But perhaps such a doctor is only releasing a patient from further interference by medical methods which have kept him or her alive beyond God's will. Who can know God's will for each soul?

Each patient should make this decision personally — and each patient, alone, will be responsible for the timing of the soul's release in death.

QUESTION: Why are there more incorruptible women saints than men after death?

ANSWER: Are there? Well, perhaps it's because women focus more thought-power on the will center, two inches below the navel — for them, the womb, because they are more children oriented. Perhaps concentrating on this navel center creates an etheric body structure more easily made incorruptible after death.

QUESTION: Why must we return? Why is a physical form necessary for the soul's liberation from the wheel of rebirth?

ANSWER: When the physical form grows old and earthly passions have died away, the soul and mind automatically revert to a subconscious longing to die, to return to the inner world for rest and rejuvenation, a release from trials and tribulations, a seeking after reward for long years of labor.

The same thing happens in reverse on the inner planes. There comes a time when the soul and mind turn again Earthward — that is, the soul who is not liberated from old karma is drawn toward rebirth through physical desires and passions not previously overcome. Although the astral form does not grow old, nevertheless, the passions of Earth not having been overcome, call the unliberated soul body-ward again. The old desires renew, memories of Earth life revive, longings for Earth possessions, longings to meet the challenges Earth represents, flexing the soul "muscles" to again enter the field of matter and conquest, the desire to incarnate with old soul friends to go through this Earth school together again. Just as the physical form gradually dies, so does the astral; and the soul — responding to the call of desires — seeks and gains rebirth.

Although this is an extreme over-simplification, it serves as a brief outline of the circumstance. Just as the Earth form is born, matures and dies, releasing the soul, just so the soul at death is born into the inner world, matures, and "dies," to be reborn on Earth. And this "second death" continues until the soul — through its own will — overcomes the desires and passions of the body. This is what Jesus meant when he admonished us to "overcome the Earth."

When it no longer responds to such desires, only then is a soul fit for liberation into higher kingdoms. The surest way of overcoming such desires is through seeking the light through studies of Wisdom teachings, initiation, prayer and meditation. Also through devotion to the Divine Current; through detachment from things of Earth and through substituting the desire for physical "union" with the desire for union with God — and this is the pathway of the saints.

Once the soul experiences union with God, the physical union pales into insignificance. The same is true of all other desires. Once the soul experiences contact with the Holy Nahd, conversion is experienced. And once conversion is experienced, liberation is assured, if the change within the consciousness continues.

QUESTION: I received a letter from a student recently. This was what she wrote: "A friend of mine is looking forward to being reunited with her parents in heaven. But how is it possible if her loved ones have reincarnated back on Earth?" Please answer it for all of us.

ANSWER: Reincarnation is a "hard" concept sometimes. You know that a lot of souls are coming back. Some have reached the high causal plane and are liberated from the wheel of rebirth. They are "saved" souls — saved from the Wheel of Rebirth and need not ever return to Earth life. Some souls do not want to return. Some look forward to it. But these saved souls need not worry about coming back unless one of them wishes to. The "cycle" is usually several thousand years. By that time the world will have experienced much evolution and have gone through some changes. But the cycle operates according to free will. It can cover anywhere from a year to five thousand years — depending on the soul's free will and the soul's karma.

But let's consider other possibilities. Let's say your son is Overthere. You want him to be there when you cross over, and you're afraid he may have incarnated. Now how in the world are you going to ever see him again if he's reincarnated? Well, let's say he has incarnated — something drew him back to Earth — he had a mission to do on Earth and he agreed to come back and fulfill it, knowing full well he would not meet you the way you expect him to when you come Overthere. Do you know you live two lives? You live your conscious life here on Earth. But at night while you sleep here, you will be fully awake Overthere, leading an entirely different life, a different home, a different group of people. You see, you are living a full life Overthere now.

Now, should that son come back to Earth as "Tom Cox," when he lived as "Jim Smith," Mr. and Mrs. "Smith" are going to be pretty anguished when they first go Overthere because their son has returned to Earth. But Jim is going to be Overthere with them every single night as his physical form sleeps. So they're going to be appeased, no matter if he does reincarnate. They are going to understand that karma brought him back and started another mission. They'll actually not miss him because they'll see him as Jim Smith each night when he is Overthere.

However, the normal pattern is for souls to stay on the inner planes for centuries, except in special cases. So don't worry that you're not going to meet your loved ones. One way or another, you'll meet and enjoy togetherness again.

QUESTION: If a New Age seeker doesn't have the advantage of the Bardo Tape* and has not yet read the Bardo Lessons, what will happen to him or her at death? (The Bardo tape is a guidance leading the dying soul into the Clear Light of salvation).

ANSWER: If he or she is a seeker, never fear. There are always those from the Otherside around the dying who will say

*Produced by Astara, Box 5003, Upland, CA 91785-5003

Death and the Soul

the words, guiding the soul into the light. They never desert a seeker in need. They meet seekers with their own type of Bardo guidance to take them into the light and make them welcome.

QUESTION: For those of us for whom it would not be appropriate to play the Bardo tape at the time of death, is there something else we can do?

ANSWER: People can pray in their own words for a welcoming of the dying soul into the realms of Light, for their negative karma to be erased and for that soul to learn any lessons necessary for them to advance spiritually, and that they be blessed with peace and love.

QUESTION: In your teachings you state it is important that the body upon death be left in quiet repose in a refrigerated room for at least 3 days to give the soul its best opportunity to experience initiation in the Clear Light or the Secondary Light.
1. What is the Clear Light or Secondary Light?
2. What is the consequence to the soul if the body does not lie in quiet repose for three days?
3. Where does one keep a body in quiet repose for 3 days?
4. What about embalming? Most states require it by law if a body is not buried immediately.

ANSWER: The questions you have posed, my beloved seeker, are those that are foremost in the minds of new initiates and deserve to be answered. Answers can be expressed briefly, but to more fully understand these subjects you should read my book, *The Mystery of Death and Dying*.

First, what is the Clear Light or Secondary Light? The Clear Light can be called the ultimate of spiritual ecstasy; or the incomparable bliss of God's Grace; or the pure White Light one sees just prior to the moment of death. It is consciousness beyond all darkness — consciousness beyond all limitations — the moment of the soul's liberation. It is salvation offered to you from the Hand of God, which may appear to be a light so dazzling that it is far beyond your perception to witness. If one is unfamiliar with the teachings of the Bardo and the Clear Light, the expanded perception may fall away and you'll not be able to hold to the Clear Light. You would eventually become conscious of the dawning of another Light — one not as brilliant as the first, but more comfortable. The Secondary Light, the light that dawns after the Clear Light fades away — the Secondary Light of Initiation — this, too, is a glorious baptism and there should be no regret about going into it.

What is the consequence to the soul if the body does not lie in quiet repose? When one goes through the death phase the body should not be disturbed at the most important moment of the just-ending incarnation — at the time the soul is looking forward to the final and highest initiation of going into the Clear Light. If the body is disturbed and the Clear Light is missed, you may miss that initiation, causing you to need to incarnate on Earth again. Following a suitable period of time after death, such as an hour or two, the body can be moved to the mortuary, to be held quietly for three days.

As to your final two questions, where does one keep a body in quiet repose for three days? At the mortuary in the "cold room." What about embalming? This should be delayed for three days, if possible. Some localities require almost immediate embalming if you are to be buried in a casket. You should speak to a local mortician and together make arrangements according

Death and the Soul

to your desires and legal requirements. You may be forced to obey the laws of embalming governing your locality, which may not allow for three days of quiet repose. But after the embalming, ask that the body be placed in a quiet place and not subjected to viewing, grief, family discussions, etc. Plan the memorial service following the three days.

If the body is to be cremated, it can be placed shortly after death in the refrigerated room for three days without embalming, and then cremated directly after removing. Thus the soul lies in quiet repose, not exposed to the disturbance of grief, body viewing, etc. — and can more easily enter the Clear Light.

QUESTION: Why are the masses of souls so afraid to die? There seems to be a built-in fear in the mass consciousness of humanity.

ANSWER: Well, simply because they've died so many times before. All of us have died many times before, and many have been very fearsome experiences. We've gone through the Valley of the Judgment, and we've met our own thoughtforms. We remember what happened to us the previous times we've died. Now that we've learned about the Bardo and the Clear Light, we want to experience a beautiful death, and that's why I've written a book on death.

But that's part of the reason the mass consciousness is afraid of dying. There is also the fear of facing the unknown. Those who aren't into the New Age don't know what's going to happen to them. They're not even sure they'll be in existence after that. A lot of people think when you're dead, you're dead. They fear there's only oblivion. That is fearsome. If I thought that, well, I'd be fearful, too. But I know better. I know about the tunnel, the Clear Light — and I know what's going to happen, so I look forward with happy anticipation to my life on the Otherside.

QUESTION: Would you recommend that when a New Age light seeker passes over, someone notify you? Do you pray for the recently deceased so their transition will be easier? How do you pray?

ANSWER: Oh, please, please do notify us at Astara — just prior to passing, or a few days before, if possible. Certainly, just following. One of my most sacred duties is to be with these special souls as they experience initiation in the White Light. Or, as they experience their first days in the higher dimensions. It is not a duty — it is rather a sacred honor. I consider it my greatest privilege to pray at that time. I link up not only with three overshadowing Masters — Rama, Zoser and Kuthumi — but also with Jesus and Mary, to the best of my ability. And to the angel world.

How do I pray? Well, I just talk to all of them — exactly as if they stood as a group before me. Then I use my own special form of a rosary to plead the Mother's help (the Flame of Love) and my own special form of the Divine Mercy Prayers when I pray to Jesus. I continue my prayers for the one gone over for at least a month following their transition. It would help, too, if, following a call, you could send a prayer petition to Astara for them. It would help us to keep a contact with them during their first month Overthere. When I am no longer here, Robert, Sita and other teachers at Astara will continue this ritual. And I hope you'll all pray for me when I, too, make my transition. And for Robert and Sita, too. Thank you.

QUESTION: Explain more about purgatory please.

ANSWER: There are many planes and phases of purgatory, just as there are many planes to heaven. The scientists are right to describe all communities of atoms as vibration — just as we light seekers are right in describing varying levels of consciousness.

Many are familiar with having one's whole life flash before one at the moment of near-death. But most are not aware that when real death does occur, this viewing of one's entire past life slows down. One emerges on the vibrational level of one's individual soul vibration. There one takes up life again. A large share of the time spent on this level of awareness will be spent in "clear viewing" or "clear reviewing" of one's past life. This time of clear viewing in the new life is called purgatory, or time of purging.

Hardly a soul enters life on the other side without spending some time in this clear viewing stage, because the soul learns so much about itself. Those who lived lives of ill deeds will surely remain longer. They will view over and over again episodes of cruelty to others, times of greed, selfishness. Nothing will be spared. This is a time of regret, remorse, hopefully repentance. They are shown what they must do to make repair, to gain forgiveness.

Those who lived ordinary lives will be shown their lives, but only to teach the soul where it could have done better, what it did wrong, what it did right. There may be regret and remorse, but not on the level of the ones who had lived with greed and ill will.

Those who lived exceptionally good lives usually still must live through the clear viewing, but each episode does not require analyzing. So the stay its brief. Some pass immediately into the higher realms without requiring a time of purging. Theirs were lives of purity and love.

For every soul in purgatory, on any level, there frequently appears a being of light offering to help, if help is sought and regret is voiced. Such help is joyfully received, except by those still bitter, still blaming others for their misfortunes, still filled with hate and revenge. These ones stay on the same level until they are ready to "see the light." Then they may be raised to higher levels of vibration in relation with their spirit form's willingness to harmonize with the level of light.

The "light people" — the average and good souls — move rapidly out of purgatory and begin their journey toward the upper planes. Their time of clear viewing will have taught the soul many needed lessons, not only of the past life, but of several previous lives, and how they are all linked together. The soul will learn whether or not it must return to mortal life again and why.

There are several planes of life in purgatory. The lower planes lie just beyond the realm of the hell planes. The upper planes lie near, and often merge with, the planes of heaven. Those who first must dwell on the lower planes are given every opportunity to move slowly upward toward the planes of heaven as they learn their lessons of love, forgiveness and enlightenment.

QUESTION: Is the body animated by a special force or energy?

ANSWER: First let us examine the discarded physical form — a form which simply "died" without injury and with no sign of disease, except perhaps that of old age. We see before us a perfectly normal creation. None of its vital parts are missing and it contains the necessary blood, but the lifeforce and the soul have fled. We find the blood standing still, and the temperature of the blood is lowered. Blood which becomes cold and stands still slowly coagulates.

Denied the life principle, the physical form becomes gradually inactive. Thus one sees before one a perfectly formed body with only one thing missing — the soul with its lifeforce. This discarded body, financially speaking, is worth approximately sixty-six cents, since all the chemical elements that compose the body may be purchased for this small amount.

The most accomplished scientist cannot create a living being from just the elements of which it is composed. Likewise, a form whose lifeforce has departed cannot again be turned into a living body. Such feats are possible only by God. Electricity will not bring the form back to life, nor will oxygen. The transition being complete, that which animated the form has fled, and science will never find a substitute for that divine substance.

That which returns to dust is the material body composed of the meager elements of Earth. The atoms which once comprised the form ultimately scatter, returning to their own levels of being. Even the discarded form is indestructible, so far as its original source — the atomic structure, or "dust" of the Earth — is concerned. The soul — the living factor — has departed for its own realms.

Chapter 5

Meditation and Soul Liberation

QUESTION: When one "sees the light" in meditation, does that mean that one is liberated from one's karma and will not need rebirth?

ANSWER: It depends upon the intensity of the search following the illumination. It certainly can mean liberation. Beginning with the incarnation when the soul first turns toward light and attunement with the Holy Nahd, the rule is that liberation is usually attained in not more than four more births. But, just as often, having once turned toward the light, all karma can be brought to an end, and the soul is liberated from the chains and desires that caused it to seek rebirth in the world of matter.

It is necessary to follow a practice of daily meditation or prayer, and guidance toward continued study of Wisdom teachings.

QUESTION: Explain how we are able to erase our karmic debts and gain liberation within four births.

ANSWER: Once the soul seeks the light, such a conversion will always remain in the consciousness, and every future birth will bring forth a subconscious memory of such a conversion.

It is indeed true that we must pay our karma, but once the soul has been converted and begins mystical studies and light seeking, the angelic forces enable us to meet and pay off our karmic debts easily, and arrange for it to be passed through within four incarnations.

Now, if a disciple follows spiritual instructions devotedly, praying, meditating to the best of one's ability, overcoming all attachments and desires of Earth, even a second time may not be required because the guardian angels, through their divine intercession, enable the remaining karma to be worked off on the inner planes, and under more favorable circumstances, or the remaining karma is simply forgiven — "the forgiveness of sins."

There are three types of karma:
1. kraya karma — meaning the deeds, thoughts and actions that we are performing here and now on a day-to-day basis, and for which we must be accountable here and now;
2. ripe karma — the karma we call fate or destiny. It is this karma that caused us to incarnate in our present birth, and it is the karma which we came to pay in this particular incarnation;
3. reserve karma — the totality of our karma, that which has been stored against us, created in many past ages, and which we have not yet been able to erase in past lives.

The normal individual, unaware of the White Light benefits of meditation, prayer or spiritual studies of Wisdom teachings, is usually creating more unpleasant karma, even while paying off previous karma. Thus there is created an unending chain of births and deaths, a labyrinth of karma out of which it is difficult to gain liberation. It is only when one turns toward light seeking and follows a prescribed course of spiritual

Meditation and Soul Liberation

discipline that one is able to cease making new karma and set to work to destroy the seeds of the old.

In his healing work Jesus frequently admonished the patient to "go and sin no more," meaning that through his power he had erased or forgiven existing karma, healed the results of the karma and freed the individual for a new path. After such an experience, if the patient sinned no more (that is, created no new karma) s/he would possess the potential for liberation here and now.

New negative karma ceases to accumulate once the disciple enters the path, since it is taken care of by the daily practice of meditation, prayer, service and following the disciplines offered in studies of the Wisdom teachings. The ripe, or fate, karma has to be faced since one has already come into the present incarnation. It is only through practicing the disciplines of initiation and the teachings of Ancient Wisdom that the disciple gains liberation.

The unwanted seeds of past karma can be destroyed through meditation and prayer. It can even lead to the wonderful transforming experience of Holy Nahd, a mystical keynote from the origin of our universe that can only be heard through meditation and prayer.

The effects of meditation and prayer are cumulative. So is following the guidelines taught in Wisdom teachings. When the seeker sets his or her face definitely in the direction of liberation, and seeks to overcome all earthly desires and attachments, the Oversoul will meet him or her more than halfway in attaining this goal.

QUESTION: Occasionally I feel a sense of fear in meditation when I experience various bodily sensations. How is one protected? How will I know when I make contact with the Holy Nahd during my meditations?

ANSWER: One is protected by first calling upon the name of the Lord and the angels of Light. After that there is nothing to be frightened about while on the inner journey. Going into the inner planes should be a delightful experience, and the disciple has no cause for fear. Besides, the inward journey only happens gradually, by degrees. Occasionally, it seems that it has happened instantaneously, but research will prove that there usually has been much prior effort before such an opening.

The disciple should overcome all fear and concentrate upon going within with full confidence that s/he is safe and secure in the Light. Fastening the attention on the Third Eye and repeating the Holy Mantra will quiet all nervousness and erase all fear.

Actually, this is the one place in all the world where one will find nothing to fear. This place within is also the only place where we can find complete peace and happiness. At the same time, when one enters the inner realms, it really is not possible to find anything there of which to be afraid, nor can one find misery and unhappiness there. All fear is self-generated and that truth is never clearer than when you are in these higher planes. Letting fear go will allow you to more closely embrace love. Gaining entrance to the inner world is like sailing into a safe harbor, a haven of rest, after being buffeted by the storms of the outer world.

Concentrating the mind upon the Third Eye is the most difficult task. It requires time and ceaseless labor. This is why it is essential to meditate regularly. As time passes, in the practice of meditation you will experience certain sensations. The

Meditation and Soul Liberation

first may appear in the lower part of the body, then in the mid-regions, and then in the head. But these are only natural and need give the disciple no cause for alarm. Once one has begun to make contact with the Holy Nahd, various sounds may be heard inside the head. Perhaps the sound of distant bells ringing, of a rushing waterfall, a swarm of buzzing bees, or the sound of hammering. These sounds mean the mind current is entering the Divine Stream toward Holy Nahd.

The best posture to hear the Holy Nahd is to sit with the knees up, with elbows on the knees and thumbs in both ears, covering the sounds of the outer world. Sitting thusly, one should turn the mind toward the center of the head, steadily breaking down all sound barriers until one enters the Divine Stream of the Holy Nahd.

It becomes possible for an advanced initiate to hear the Sound of the Nahd constantly — subdued, of course. A powerful sound of the Nahd would be distracting if it were heard at full volume, making it impossible to turn one's attention outward to worldly duties. Such a condition is not desirable.

QUESTION: You used to teach us to focus our minds on OM MANI PADME HUM during our meditations, until your vision of the Blessed Virgin in the Great Pyramid. After that you said that we could say the rosary. Which is the more powerful of the chants?

ANSWER: When I was told to switch over and say the rosary, that was traumatic for me because I could not understand how saying those words and holding a set of beads could possibly do for me what OM MANI PADME HUM had done for so many years. But I had been told to do it, and I was determined to follow directions and to suggest it to others. I knew there had to be a reason, so I sought my answer and received it. Now let me see if I can share it appropriately.

OM MANI PADME HUM — Ma is the Mother. So with OM MANI PADME HUM you have a universal chant. Beautiful, very, very powerful. So along comes "Hail Mary full of Grace, the Lord is with thee. Blessed art Thou among women, blessed is the fruit of Thy womb, Jesus. Holy Mary, Mother of God, pray for us now and pour the grace of your Flame of Love upon the whole of mankind now and at the hour of our death." So, I'm supposed to say that? Why? Give me a reason.

The reason is very, very simple and very, very beautiful. There came a time when we were just entering the ethers of the Aquarian Age. You see, the ethers surrounding the globe at that particular time were, and still remain, focused more on the masculine side of the masculine/feminine polarity.

In 1917 the Mother appeared to three little children in Fatima, Portugal. Jesus told little Jacinta, one of the children, "You must tell the people that I am stepping back now in order for them to bring through the New Age and world peace through my mother. Through Mary to Jesus." Mary then began coming forward with tremendous force to the feminine side of the male/female polarity to balance the masculine-feminine ethers, the polarity throughout and around this planet. And who is to do that but the Divine Mother?

I realized then that my task in suggesting that you say the rosary was not to turn you toward a certain faith or religion, but to bring down through her the feminine ethers, so that we can balance the Earth polarity at this particular time, and bring the New Age into being. And that is her purpose. Not so that we can bring her personal adoration; she doesn't need that. She has all the adoration she needs. But she is the person, the feminine divinity, through whom we will bring the New Age into proper focus. She is the feminine Light of the World. And in calling upon the rosary we are pulling down through her the feminine ethers we need so badly now.

If you prefer to continue saying the OM mantra, that's fine. It's still a powerful universal cosmic chant. If you choose the rosary, you need not repeat the words of the traditional rosary. Select your own formula, one which appeals to you. But do focus your attention upon the Blessed Virgin. My own choice is this: first I say the creed, "I believe in God, the Father Almighty, etc.; then second, I say the Salva Regina, then Our Father which art in heaven (the Lord's Prayer), then I say the Hail Mary. This breaks the monotony of repeating the traditional rosary prayer and offers unequaled prayer potency.

QUESTION: Sometimes it seems that the moment one becomes a disciple on the path, difficulties increase. Would you please comment?

ANSWER: It is easy to see the difficulties through which one has to pass, but one is never aware of what one had been spared. As meditation and prayers become increasingly intense, you will become aware that the difficulties are actually challenges to be met and conquered. Problems are not really problems, but opportunities.

You will also become aware that your spiritual efforts may be rewarding you in that you are being spared many difficulties which might have come your way. Small miracles begin to happen in your daily life — suddenly finding a lost object; a minor or major accident avoided; an unexpected blessing of nature.

QUESTION: Does it help to speak of your inner experiences to others?

ANSWER: No. As a general rule, the disciple should not share his or her inward journeys with other people. There are exceptions, of course, but the disciple should be extremely discerning in sharing such experiences. Speaking of them constantly and among those who may not understand is "casting your pearls before swine." Such foolish chatter can dissipate power that is needed for more successful meditations. If, however, you speak to others who support you, are like-minded and respect your path, this can be helpful. Make sure to avoid feeling that you must talk to others about every experience in order for it to be validated in some way. Sometimes it is important to "hold these things in your heart."

QUESTION: Can you suggest a prayer of dedication for us to close our meditations?

ANSWER: After your quiet period of meditation, raise your hands above the head in the sign of the chalice, with the hands cupped. In a spirit of supplication with the hands up and the face raised to heaven, repeat this prayer:

"Master of love and compassion, I am dedicated to Thy service. I approach Thee in faith in the White Light force, the unseen companion of the heart. Prepare me, O Lord, to drink of the living waters of life, soon to be made manifest unto me. Open my eyes that I may see, and my heart that I may understand. Make the way plain, O Lord, that I fail not in Thy service. May I be a channel whereby the Holy Ones may approach the world. May I be a center of radiation of Thy power.

And teach me to travel light, giving myself entirely to Thy service, attuning myself to Thy will, laying down the small personal life for the great cosmic life, and loving with the love of God."

This ceremony should be performed especially on the night of the full moon, and on the night of the new moon.

QUESTION: Often when I meditate, in Padmasan posture, I experience a numbness of the extremities, especially the feet and legs. Should I terminate meditation when this happens?

ANSWER: No. Numbness of the extremities is the result of the consciousness being withdrawn from body awareness. It is a sign of progress. Such a condition is only temporary, and should not be a cause of alarm. However, if the feet and legs become painful, stop the meditation and move about to restore the circulation. Perhaps it is better for you to avoid Padmasan posture and sit in a straight chair which will support your back.

QUESTION: Why is it important to turn the attention to the Third Eye center in meditation?

ANSWER: The Third Eye is the window, or doorway to the spiritual world, and the best passageway the mind or soul has in contacting the Oversoul in meditations. The other nine openings of the body turn outward to the lower world of matter. Through the Third Eye, or concentration on the tip of the nose, the disciple more easily ascends to the celestial regions and unites with God.

QUESTION: Regular meditation and spiritual studies seem to erase all fears of death. Can you explain this?

ANSWER: True and deep meditation is actually a form of death. The consciousness withdraws from the physical form and becomes attuned to the inner worlds and the Oversoul. A sincere light seeker need never fear death. Meditation only brings about an actual understanding of the initiation of the death experience.

Those who meditate regularly, who have constantly repeated the cosmic mantra, or who have prayed much, are taken to higher regions immediately when they depart the body. They have established an esoteric, etheric link-up with their guardian angels. Their angels of Light always come at the time of death, to carry these souls through the doorway of initiation, and take them to higher planes.

If such a disciple has been able to overcome worldly desires s/he will not likely find it necessary to seek rebirth in this world. It is the natural inclination of the spirit to join the Father/Mother in heaven. It is the mind, enthralled with earthly phenomena and pleasures, which creates karmic conflict that draws the soul back to rebirth. Only through proper meditation and prayer can the mind be brought under control, thus freeing the soul to journey forever to the higher regions, gaining liberation from the wheel of rebirth.

Those who have an innate fear of death are the souls who are remembering past deaths when they experienced the Lonesome Valley of the Bardo, due to past unpleasant karma. Those with good karma only experience the White Light during the Bardo journey, and those who — because of prayer — entered the protecting and guiding influence of the Holy Nahd form of the Oversoul, need never fear death.

In the deeps of meditation, riding the stream of the Sound Current, there is no pain, no death, no illness. There is only love and light, and the radiant form of the divine Oversoul. If one learns how to "die" while still in the body, one will never have to be born and die again.

QUESTION: What do you mean by Darshan in meditation?

ANSWER: A spiritual Master, angel or teacher is one who guides the disciple, not only in outer life but from the inner planes, once the disciple is able to intuit the Oversoul during meditations, or through the disciplines of the study of Wisdom teachings and initiation.

During such studies and disciplines, the mind should be kept firmly fixed upon the Oversoul, with the hope of experiencing Holy Darshan, which means to see the Master's or the guardian angel's face in a vision, and to communicate through the Sound Current of Holy Nahd. This is Darshan.

In such a meditation the attention should be concentrated at the center between the eyes — the Third Eye. It is from the center of the Third Eye that the inward journey begins. Centering the attention here concentrates the scattered thoughts, and focuses them on one doorway through which the mind and soul are drawn upward through the Sound Current.

QUESTION: What is gained by Jap — the repetition of the cosmic mantra?

ANSWER: "Knock and it shall be opened unto you." You are familiar with this quotation. Jap, or repetition, means knocking at the door of the Third Eye, repeating — repeating — repeating, is knocking ... knocking ... knocking at the inner barrier. As the repetition is continued it gains in power until it batters down the barrier, the doorway, and the disciple enters the inner realm, there to confront the radiant form of a guardian angel, the Clear Light, or even our Mother/Father God.

One must first withdraw the consciousness from the outer world, then center it upon the Third Eye and the mantra. Such an inner journey may be long and arduous, since the quieting of the mind is one's greatest challenge. Placing the thumbs over the front part of the ears helps to close off outer sounds and focus the thoughts inward. The challenge then is to send the thought force inward, beating against the barrier until one enters the inner realms.

The point is to begin, to remain regular, and not to become discouraged. Actually, each meditation should spur the disciple to more intense efforts. Discouragement should never manifest, for every meditation is progress, even though the disciple may not be aware of it. And every meditation brings the disciple nearer to the center, and contact with the Nahd.

Each meditation should find the disciple experiencing greater inner peace, a subtle joy, the unfolding of a great inner power, and a spiritual awareness. He or she will also experience a burning love for God and all one's fellow creatures.

QUESTION: Is it correct to practice Jap (repetition) in rhythm with the breathing?

ANSWER: Each disciple is free to choose their own method. Some repeat the mantra with each inhalation and exhalation, while some repeat the mantra giving no thought to the breath whatever. Each is correct.

It is better not to concentrate upon the breathing if it causes the attention to wander from repetition of the mantra. The repetition should come first. If repetition can be achieved without even thinking of the breath in any way, this is the superior method. However, the breath should be as quiet and inconspicuous as possible without giving too much effort toward it.

QUESTION: Describe some of the sensations that may be experienced during advanced meditation.

ANSWER: Some of the sensations are visual and auditory, although the initial dominant sensations will be what you feel on your skin. There may come the sensation of spiders crawling about the face and body. Although irritating, this is nothing to which to give attention. There may also come the feeling of pinpricks. This again is normal, and no cause for alarm. This is only the essence of Kundalini stirring in answer to the vibration of chanting or thought current.

The body may sway occasionally, as if being pushed forward and backward by some inner force. One should not attempt to hold the body firm, unless such a rocking diverts attention from Jap and dyhana. When the attention is properly focused at the Third Eye, you will witness some lights, pinpoints, flashes or swirls. These are excellent signs of progress. Auditory sensations are generally the sounds of rushing waters, the chiming of bells, a subtle buzzing of bees, or a distant flute.

QUESTION: I have been told that it is far more important to serve others than it is to spend time in meditation. Would you please advise?

ANSWER: Doing as much as possible for others is very beautiful, and most certainly should be done in the course of a human lifetime. But the entire meaning and purpose of human incarnation is to free the soul to return to God. Meditation, Jap and prayer are the vital, spiritual works of incarnation that can be given potency by serving others, allowing the soul to unite with God, our Supreme Father/Mother in Heaven. There are many other life experiences, however, that also give power and force to this vital work. These experiences are all part of the process of a soul's evolution, but they are not more important than the spiritual work. Each should make one's own choice of how best to attain soul salvation.

> Three doors there are to the temple —
> To work, to serve, to pray;
> And those who wait at the outer gate
> May enter by either way.

QUESTION: You have said that it is possible to see the face of a Master or spiritual guide when one enters deeply into meditation, and that it is possible, once one has contacted the Holy Nahd, to hear the voice of a Master or spiritual guide speak, advising and guiding you. Is it also possible to see the Master Jesus under such circumstances?

ANSWER: It most assuredly is. When present day disciples of Christ declare they have seen His face or His form, it is always in His radiant form of Holy Nahd. A Master such as

Meditation and Soul Liberation

Jesus never appears in the materialized physical form. It is always in the spiritual, Nahd form. And He assuredly will appear when the disciple has so prepared his or her mind. His voice can be heard speaking once the consciousness has penetrated the audible life stream of the Holy Nahd. This is also true of other avatars such as Buddha, Moses or any of those we call the Ascended Masters.

QUESTION: Does the disciple actually see a Master face to face in meditation when he or she has successfully contacted Holy Nahd?

ANSWER: When the disciple is able to enter deeply into the Third Eye and reach the center, only then does he or she see the Master or spiritual guide face to face. But at that time one most assuredly does. Not only does one come face to face with the being, but one is able to hear a voice, guiding, advising, loving, and protecting him or her. The voice may be inaudible to the consciousness, but the subconscious and the superconscious will surely absorb its message. This is true Darshan.

Whether or not you ever see your Master, you must know this Master is always within, and though you may be unaware of it, sees all your actions.

QUESTION: Sometimes it seems that during the early practice of meditation unusually negative, disruptive, sexual, and even evil thoughts crowd into the consciousness. What is happening? Suddenly I'm filled with fear — afraid the unseen teachers will be aware of my sexual or negative thoughts. Can you please explain what is taking place?

ANSWER: This again is the action of the mind, the past thoughtforms which we call our personal "devil(s)," and the ego attempting to distract you. When this happens, open the eyes and for a few moments think of something else, willing the disruptive thoughts away. If necessary, rise and walk around for a few moments, chanting your cosmic mantra aloud. This will usually set the mind on the right path again.

Do not allow these disruptive thoughts to disturb you personally. They are not "yours," except that they belong to the stream of thoughtforce created by you in the past, or they have drifted in from the mass consciousness of the plane upon which you now manifest. Do not make such thoughts a part of yourself, and do not become anxious or concerned about them, or worried that a Master may observe their presence. Adopt an attitude of indifference about them. Do not become attached to them through fear or shame. Let them flow away as easily as they have come, and continue your meditations.

QUESTION: Sometimes it is difficult to find the time to meditate or pray. Does this mean that the disciple loses ground in his or her attaining?

ANSWER: Just as a pianist loses skill when practice is not faithful, so does the disciple lose meditative skills when practice is not regular. When we make appointments with business acquaintances and friends, we are always prompt in attending to them. Why can we not always do the same with our inner, divine self? Just as one should not neglect worldly duties and obligations, neither should regular meditation be neglected. Our spiritual growth is far more important than the other activities, and is imperative if one seeks to attain

Meditation and Soul Liberation

liberation. It is understandable that one must occasionally miss prayer time, but return to schedule as soon as possible — and try to make it at the same time daily, even if only for five minutes.

QUESTION: Why is it so difficult to center the mind and concentrate on one thing? The mind seems like the proverbial monkey, always leaping from one thought to another.

ANSWER: Concentration only comes through long effort, but no effort is ever wasted. You must remember that it may have been many generations, many incarnations, many centuries, perhaps even ages, that your mind has been allowed free rein with no restraint whatever. It will require concentrated effort to still it and have it obey your will.

As the mind learns deeper and deeper concentration, so also will sound become increasingly obvious. Your feeling of frustration will gradually abate, as your inner awareness sharpens. Remember this: no effort is ever lost. Some gain is made during every meditation, though the disciple may experience only disappointment.

It is important also to be aware that when the disciple begins regular meditation and attempts to contact the Nahd, the mind and ego will also become increasingly active, actually seeking to prevent the attention from centering inward.

Not only is it possible to meditate in the midst of a crowd during social activities, but you should cultivate the habit of practicing Jap at any other time when you are not actually engaged in conversations with others or in performing your duties. Any time you are riding in a car, on public transportation, taking a bath, or practicing any occupation that does not require your full attention, although it may not be possible to adopt your usual meditation posture, nor close your eyes, still the attention can be centered at the Third Eye, and repetition of the mantra practiced.

It should be remembered that the principal reason you came into incarnation was to learn to still the mind, and attune to the Nahd. Incarnation is always precious, and every opportunity should be sought to unite with God. Every possible moment you can spare from your earthly duties should be so spent. Only thus will you learn how to take the mind on the inward journey for liberation, thus completing your round of births and deaths.

One should also learn to meditate and go within while lying in bed. It is an excellent practice prior to sleep. It turns the attention from the without to the within, and in time such a practice becomes habit. Since the very reason we have come into incarnation is to enable us to realize God within ourselves, this constant meditation is a most desirable habit.

QUESTION: Is it suitable when meditating to concentrate upon a favorite photograph of one's chosen Master, Avatar or spiritual guide?

ANSWER: There is no better method. Focus your attention on his or her Third Eye area and hold it there. Constantly repeat the cosmic mantra, OM MANI PADME HUM, or your own mantra or form of the rosary, taking the mind in and up through such repetition. The Master, Avatar or spiritual guide may "come alive" in living, speaking form.

I remember when this once happened to me — unexpectedly. I was attending an "intensive training" seminar held in

Berkeley, California, conducted by the famous late guru Muktananda. I was sitting among his special disciples grouped near the dais upon which he sat in his throne-chair. Above his head hung a picture of his guru. Another hung on the wall of the hall directly across from where I sat. I could look directly into the eyes of his guru (I have forgotten his name).

As the meeting progressed, I was suddenly attracted to the eyes of Muktananda's guru and froze in astonishment as I saw them actually "come alive." Then just as suddenly, the face and eyes of Jesus overshadowed those of the guru. He was gazing straight into my eyes. Then the face and eyes began to move toward me, closer and closer.

I wasn't frightened — just paralyzed with the intensity of his image. As His face moved toward me, I knew without doubt His face and eyes were going to merge into my own face and eyes. I felt an indescribable power about to envelope my head as His image, His eyes, were focused with mine.

As His face and eyes merged with mine, the entire hall and its surroundings faded into a foggy mist. My head opened up with the enveloping power. I heard Him speak inside my head. He said, "Am I not enough for thee, little one?"

Then the power faded away. My head returned to normal. But I never did — and I never shall. I left the seminar as soon as possible. No more longing for a guru. I had found my own. Closer and closer have I drawn to my own guru, Jesus. He truly is all I need, and through Him I have found a profound peace and cosmic fulfillment. The light of His image, the sound of His voice, have never left me. I only wait to meet Him face to face and say to Him, "You are all I need."

Each of you can find your own Master or Teacher, whose teachings will lead you to discover your own inner divinity. This is of the utmost importance.

QUESTION: How can the disciple be sure a Master or angel is aware of one's meditations if there is no apparent evidence?

ANSWER: It was concerning this query that the Master Jesus spoke when he said, "Seek and ye shall find; knock and it shall be opened."

Regardless of the circumstances, you may be very sure that any being is aware of the disciple who is knocking at the door. Whether that Master or angel is a living guru, or a Master from spirit, the seeker who meditates is never alone in his or her meditations. The fact that there is no manifestation of a presence signifies only that the seeker is not yet capable of discerning a presence, not that the presence is absent.

The very fact that one longs for Darshan (an inner vision of the Master) is in itself enough to draw the attention of the Master. When such a longing becomes intense, the Master answers it in some way, though the disciple is not always aware. As the intensity of meditation increases, the disciple may experience a desire to spend more time in meditation and study and to avoid trivial social activities. Some outside duties, however, cannot be avoided. For such a disciple it is important to know that even in the midst of a crowd one can occasionally practice Jap.

Once you have contacted Holy Nahd, you will never feel lonely again.

QUESTION: It is understandable that one can more easily handle loneliness, but what of the cosmic loneliness — how does one handle that?

ANSWER: In the final analysis, you are really always alone until you complete your rounds of births and deaths, finally

Meditation and Soul Liberation

uniting with God. Until that time, however, you have to realize that you came alone into the world; you are alone in your spiritual meditations, and when you leave this world you shall walk the Lonesome Valley of the Bardo alone.

You will only find surcease from the pain of this cosmic aloneness by attunement to the Holy Nahd. Only attunement to the Sound brings the peace of mind your soul seeks, until you reach completion and become one with God.

But, spending time in prayer, meditation and with other like-minded Seekers can ease the loneliness a great deal.

QUESTION: How is Lhama Yoga of The Penetralia different from other yoga?

ANSWER: Most yoga involves some form of action, whereas Lhama Yoga is mostly mental. Breath is involved in the beginning, but ultimate success lies in the listening yoga. That is what Lhama Yoga truly is — a listening yoga, a yoga of the stillness, a yoga of longing and eventual fulfillment.

It is also the best discipline for entering the Holy Nahd Sound Current. This is done by placing the thumbs in the ears to close off outer sounds and concentrating the mind energy on entering the head center. This is the heart of Lhama Yoga, a method of yoga taught by certain teachers of the order of Melchizedek.

QUESTION: Why is it important in meditation to concentrate upon repetition of the cosmic mantra or some word?

ANSWER: The object of all yoga, especially the yoga of the mind, is to disassociate the mind from the sense organs, to still the constant motion of the mind by concentration. Fastening the attention upon a particular mantra leads to intense concentration of the mind, and causes it to become increasingly aware of the inner universe. Because mind is always in constant motion and can never become a complete blank, the best way to serve its busyness is to apply it to concentration upon a given word or mantra.

Such contemplation causes an awareness of the more subtle senses. Success in such contemplation can only be gained through the use of the subtle senses. As the attention is turned within, concentration deepens. Beauty is often seen and sounds are often heard through the causal senses. Continued practice brings detachment from all mind and matter, making the High Self, which possesses all knowledge, accessible. Continued contemplation causes the mind to become completely still, bringing the Sound Current of the Holy Nahd into action.

QUESTION: Please speak further about meditation in the context of the experiences one may have and how to interpret them.

ANSWER: "Sanskari" souls are those who have made contact with the light through meditation in a previous life. Such souls are easily recognized by Masters, whether the Master is living, or in spirit. Such souls usually come into rebirth overshadowed by a great Master, teacher or an angel from the inner planes, and will answer the call to a "discipleship" through the influence of the unseen being.

Even so, it remains for him or her to live through their fate karma, or their destiny — the karma which brought them to their present incarnation. But once the disciple begins meditations and

Jap (repetition of a chant), such a destiny is made easier. It should be remembered that although the spiritual guide can give instructions in spiritual discipline, and even put the soul in touch with Holy Nahd, it remains for the disciple to personally make the effort to reach the Light through his or her own meditations. Only the disciple can draw the consciousness to the Third Eye center, and practice Jap. All that is truly needed to complete the spiritual journey is faith, time and perseverance.

With the faith comes a loving surrender to a higher power. Time and perseverance brings the desired reward. One should spend from 20 minutes to an hour when possible going within to the Third Eye and repeating the Cosmic Mantra. If Jap interferes with listening, then discontinue Jap. When the Sound begins to be heard, one should listen to the Sound intently for at least 20 minutes. When the Sound begins to act as a magnet, pulling you upward, you should yield to the magnetic pull. Cease repeating the mantra, and listen ... listen ... listen ... following after the Sound.

In other words, focus on listening, and yield to the inward pulling current of the Sound. The time will come when you will experience Holy Darshan, that is, you will witness the Radiant Form of a Master or angel after listening intently to the Sound.

Sensations while meditating ...

It sometimes happens that during meditation one sees various forms, often distorted and unpleasant. Again, this is no cause for alarm. One is simply witnessing one's own distorted thoughtforms. All thoughts of any intensity build thoughtforms. Many of them are distorted because they have not been perfectly created. They reflect the eternal turbulent motion of the mind, which moves from thought to thought, usually never completing any one of them.

The disciple should view these visions with indifference, letting them flow in and out without any alarm. Thus they pass out of consciousness and out of viewing range to become dissipated. Concentration upon the Third Eye and Jap will dispel all such thought forms. Practicing Jap is not solely for the purpose of breaking the habit of the mind to wander. The major purpose is to arouse spiritual vibrations within, which open the physical form, enabling it to come in contact with the downpouring Sound Current.

Constant meditation and Jap create centers in the brain. As with all areas of the brain, these centers are strengthened with use, and it becomes easier and easier to focus attention within. Repeating the Cosmic Mantra over and over is like cutting a record with a fine needle. It eventually becomes a mental habit, easier and easier to accomplish each time it is attempted.

Once Nahd is contacted, the disciple realizes that the best things this Earth has to offer are as nothing compared to the joy and bliss of such a contact.

QUESTION: Once one has opened the Third Eye and seen the Radiant Form of the being within, during meditations, does this imply that all karma has been dissipated?

ANSWER: No. Some disciples contact the Radiant Form or the Clear Light right in their beginning meditations. It is how they conduct their daily lives afterward that is important. But should there be remaining karma after an experience in the Clear Light, the Oversoul — aware of the disciple's devotion — may guide the disciple into circumstances and situations so that the karma may be more easily dissipated and the disciple need not be born again.

This can only happen when the disciple overcomes pronounced desires or attachments. If such a liberation is not possible in one lifetime, the disciple — coming again into rebirth — will enter under highly desirable (spiritual) circumstances with an enlightened mind and great spiritual opportunities. The incarnation should be a complete blessing, not only to the disciple, but to all humankind.

QUESTION: How long should the disciple meditate?

ANSWER: From twenty minutes to as long as possible, depending on one's circumstances and environment. Regularity is also extremely important. Meditation is a spiritual practice. You receive the greatest benefit when you can sit for twenty minutes once or twice a day at the same time each day. Whenever this is not possible, don't give it up altogether. Even five minutes at anytime is better than not practicing at all because even five minutes can bring you in touch with that cosmic sea of divine consciousness.

The Sound Current is always there, whether one meditates half an hour, or half a day. The Sound cannot be lost. It is only the attention to it that is lost. The Sound may only come when the mind is freed from worries and anxieties, and can be held serene and tranquil. Otherwise, the Sound may recede into the background and appear to be lost altogether, but such is not possible. The Sound can strike the brain with such suddenness that it briefly stops all activity.

In the beginning of a meditation much of the time is consumed in overcoming the restlessness of the mind, and fixing the attention upon the Third Eye and Jap. This is why it is desirable to have one extended meditation rather than several shorter ones. Much time is required to still the mind, but the more time that is given, the easier the meditation becomes.

As one perseveres, the consciousness becomes more and more oriented inward. And after the disciple once hears the Nahd, s/he begins to experience the feeling of the Sound hovering over and around almost constantly.

QUESTION: What are the disciplines to follow to attain initiation?

ANSWER: The processes of enlightenment are the result of very simple changes. It is a matter of maturing certain sensations, thoughts and qualities which are dormant in all, but which must be awakened. But only those who carry these simple processes to fulfillment, with patience, diligence and love can expect any illumination.

Out of meditation the organs for functioning on the inner planes are developed. Inner sight is awakened, consciousness of higher levels of contact are unfolded, and gradually the candidate is prepared for actual initiation itself. These organs may be called spiritual eyes, or the Third Eye. It helps you to see on the inner planes, to become aware of the vibrations of those higher levels and to utilize the teachings which are given you there.

When you reach the stage where the Spiritual Eyes are opened, much lies before you. You are not yet fully developed, but you are well started on the way, and from that point forward may choose which of the aspects of development you wish to concentrate upon. If you have passed through the initial stages

Meditation and Soul Liberation

of development, from the first step of curious interest to actual awakening, you have already proven your endurance, your courage and your sincerity. The gifts of the spirit are yours, but you still are responsible for using them correctly and constructively, for yourself and your fellow creatures.

The question as to whether you are preparing correctly for initiation involves several things. First, you must be sure your physical organism is prepared. Usually, those who start out on the pathway are well fortified in this respect; they are careful of the physical body, they do not use it recklessly, for as long as it is the temple of the higher vehicles it must be tended and cared for, just as one would a machine which is valuable and delicately constructed. The physical body is the machine which is used by the higher vehicles to manifest on the Earth plane, and, of course, must be protected and nurtured that it may at all times operate with as complete efficiency as possible. This does not mean good health — even the greatest initiates have experienced physical problems — it means avoiding undesirable habits which contaminate the physical form, such as tobacco, intoxicating drinks, drugs or an impure diet.

The second consideration is the ability to concentrate and use these forces of meditation in a constructive manner. All who are successful in the business world, all who are successful in the scientific world or in the arts, must necessarily know how to concentrate. If concentration is so necessary for success on the material plane, how very much more essential is it for the development of the higher faculties! So when the Mystery Schools teach concentration, and recommend it as necessary for the mystical pathway, they are automatically training you in developing control of the higher vehicles, and at the same time teaching you a practical, useful exercise that can be employed for betterment on the physical plane.

Concentration means the elimination of superfluous ideas and thoughts. It is cultivating the quality to do one thing at a time, and to do that thing well. We cannot scatter our activities and expect to become efficient in any of them. But if we can direct all of our vitality into each thing we do, giving each activity, whether it is a temporary or a permanent one, the benefit of our complete attention, our work is easier, more exact and more satisfying.

Now the use of concentration in psychic or spiritual work has the same effect. We learn to turn within, to spiritually and mentally focus the consciousness on an illuminating, enlightening point of interest. In doing so we concentrate our spiritual energy to that focal point.

As you progress, first you may only have a few seconds of actual "realization." Later on, this period may be extended to a full minute. As time passes, and as your daily life gives you further advantage of training in practical objectives, you find your inner powers increasing in proportion to your intellectual and practical understanding of inner truths to everyday life. Then there comes the time when you are freed from the Wheel of Birth and Death, and proceed from Earth to inner plane activity, exclusive of the physical level.

The third point to be considered is the development of all the qualities necessary for such initiation. We know that in scholastic work it is necessary that the child or student maintain a certain average if he or she expects to pass examinations. Certain fundamental necessary subjects are assigned to each class of students, and they must pass the average grade in each of these if they are to hope for promotion. Usually, this grade is well within the grasp of any who will apply themselves to these subjects.

It is necessary that they have a fundamental knowledge of

arithmetic, grammar, spelling, history, literature, music, etc., even though personal preference may not include one or more of these subjects. We would not consider the student educated if he or she finished school without having at least a rudimentary knowledge of all these topics. They are part of our cultural system.

It is so with training for initiation — we can't expect to enter into the inner planes as a qualified initiate if we haven't passed through the various problems associated with that development and solved all of them in at least a satisfactory manner. We can't expect a deep desire for initiation to, in itself, be all that is necessary, any more than we would expect the student's delight in the prospect of graduating from the primary grades to be all that is necessary for his or her promotion.

Besides the desire to complete one's work, the student must also prove an ability to proceed, and actually undertake subjects or duties which are not entirely pleasant. Completing these less-favored subjects is in itself a vital element of training, for wherever we may go we must learn to see all sides of a question, we must learn to temper our own desires with the needs and necessities of others; we must learn the value of sacrifice for the good of some higher aspiration and ideal.

In initiation we are not assigned any particular subjects. Nevertheless, the general qualifications are the same as those used in the educational system. The candidate may have an abounding love for humanity, but if that love is not tempered with good judgment and discrimination, then these qualities must be developed. On the other hand, if the candidate has shown a desire to develop in the qualities of control and understanding, then the abundance of love which that candidate has attained will help to equalize one's general standard of development. And so on through all of the traits of character necessary for initiation.

QUESTION: Can you tell us more about entering the Temple of Wisdom?

ANSWER: In entering the inner plane Temple of Wisdom, some offering must be made. There is no fee levied in monetary terms; the only offering we can make is ourselves. The more developed we are, the more acceptable our gifts become, for initiation implies the opportunity to develop still greater faculties, and the opportunity to serve in a larger capacity. The more highly developed we are, the more useful our services will be in the inner plane realms.

There is no point in our going empty-handed to such an inner plane Temple, for there are many things that can be learned here on the Earth plane. Our incarnation has been given us for the purpose of learning them. To attempt to storm the doors of the inner planes without having cultivated the qualities we were sent to Earth to develop is very much like a child demanding his/her certificate of graduation without having attended the necessary educational classes. The opportunity for such education is open to everyone, just as the opportunity for soul development is given to everyone on the Earth plane.

No matter where we may be, there are abounding chances for study, for concentrating upon life's problems, for becoming more aware of nature, her forces and her influences. Whether we live in the city or in the country, each offers its characteristic advantages; whether our financial status is high or low, we have, in the state we are in, opportunities which are denied those in other phases of environment. All of these things are parts of our chances for observation.

In effect, when we indicate our desire to study the inner plane laws through mystical work and writings, we are presenting ourselves at the door of the inner plane Temple —

Meditation and Soul Liberation 109

sometimes untrained and undisciplined. Therefore, we must prepare ourselves before we can expect entry. Actual, active, direct mystical study is one half of this training; practical observation of life is the other half.

But, of course, there is a great variety in the qualifications of the initiate, just as there is a great variety in the qualifications of any specialized science. It is quite possible for an entire class of graduates in science, for instance, to receive the same scientific degree. Some will have barely passed their examinations. Others will have had brilliant academic careers. Initiates, then, have just as varied qualifications as such Earth plane class members. The more highly developed the candidate, the more useful his or her services will be.

So, we can understand, therefore, this mystery of initiation occurring at so many different stages in the lives of seekers. One who has had a rather mediocre life, who has never shown any brilliant capacity for any particular mystical phase of endeavor, or philosophical understanding, may, because their development has been well-rounded and balanced, receive one of the beginning initiatory experiences. Though no brilliant achievement has occurred, a sound, fundamental understanding of esoteric principles has developed.

On the other hand, there are many competent scholars, many who have distinguished themselves in several phases of esoteric activity and have passed far beyond what we would ordinarily consider necessary for initiation, yet they are still without that sublime experience. It is evident that in such cases some small impediment has prevented their development, some fundamental basic necessity for entry into full understanding of the inner planes has prevented their initiation.

It is necessary that they wait, therefore, until these needed traits are nurtured, and while doing so their capacity along other lines in which they are already proficient proceeds to an even greater level. When they are finally initiated, they will, in every respect, be just as highly developed as those who may have been initiated many years, or many lifetimes ahead of them.

QUESTION: Would you please tell me what Rukraksha and Tulsi Mala beads are that you mentioned in some of your writings?

ANSWER: Mala beads are brown beads from the Rukraksha tree, which grows in India. Many gurus wear them constantly, but especially during prayer time. They count their chants on the beads just as we Westerners use the beads of the rosary. Mine, given me by a guru from India, has 54 beads on it, plus one central bead, making a total of 55. I'm not sure if all mala beads bear the same number, but I'm sure they should just as all rosaries total the same number of beads.

QUESTION: Is it alright to say both the OM and the Rosary?

ANSWER: Both the OM and the Rosary are excellent ways to balance the energies of the East and West. If you wish to say the OM, you might better say the OM MANI PADME HUM — because then you are including the mother force. If you say the OM on the rosary, you should also say something concerning the feminine polarity. You can certainly say both. You don't even need to say the traditional rosary.

Many people, including myself, have difficulty saying the traditional rosary over and over because one loses one's concentration. That's alright as long as one says something that

Meditation and Soul Liberation

will bring down the feminine polarity. The OM alone is masculine. So if you say just the OM, you're not indrawing any of the feminine polarity. So do find something feminine to balance it with, even if its just OM MANI. If you don't want to say both, just say OM MA, which includes the Mother force.

QUESTION: Can you give us a scientific, or medical, or even spiritual reason you keep urging us to say the rosary? How can a string of beads heal or save a soul?

ANSWER: Well, let's talk about it again. Now, here's this human body. We have often talked about the magnetic power of the body. Every cell in this body is a tiny power plant. Our bodies are also electric, thus making our bodies electromagnetic. With our minds we create a forcefield around us — an electromagnetic forcefield. Do you know when you cup your hands you are forming another forcefield? You can feel it. Around your own hands you can feel a forcefield. If you put your palms together and just lightly part them, you can feel a force there.

Well, now let's discuss chanting. The yogis teach the disciple to sit in the Padmasan lotus posture and chant OM-OM-OM — until your neighbors wish you would go to India. That repetition is called Japa or Jap (the last "a" is usually silent). There is little doubt as to the power of that chant. It is so powerful that a different resonance begins to take place in our bodies. The cells begin to fill with a new energy and enzymes become more active, depending on the force of our minds.

Now when we create this energy with the chant of the rosary beads, we're also creating a forcefield. When we say "Hail Mary, full of grace, the Lord is with Thee," with reverence and love for this great Lady, a forcefield of White Light is established. You must feel it for it to be effective. You must create the forcefield with a reverential love to establish a healing. You must also pour out the White Light energy into your hands.

The repetition of some aspect of the rosary will cause changes because of the reverence. Your reverence will cause the healing because your hands are like magnets. It's the changing of the magnetic fields of the world now that are bringing in the New Age.

Saying the rosary can change history. As an example, let's presume there are two possible outcomes from a catacylsmic event. Now for the positive outcome supported by the rosary, picture thousands of us with our rosaries and we chant, chant and chant together. Now we all believe in the great power of that chant — but it's the thought and sound force, and the electromagnetic energy generated by the reverence of our physical energy that's going to help determine the results of the cataclysmic event. The magnetism of the sound of the chant rises and molds immense powerful forms of thoughtforce. Now the Blessed Mother will not directly interfere, but she can enhance the power of that cloud of magnetism, that cloud of White Light rising from all the dedicated praying souls. That thoughtforce begins to affect the outcome of the event. Which way do you think it will go? Do you think it possible to affect our futures in this way? It certainly is possible.

So using your own personal formula with the rosary is urged because it can change the auric forcefield and cause the White Light to radiate outward into vast areas. Unseen forces using this power can project it ever outward to purify incredible space. When many pray the rosary simultaneously, the White Light from each, flowing upward and outward, can link together to destroy much dark thoughtforce and purify vast

Meditation and Soul Liberation

realms. To repeat, one need not even say the traditional rosary — which may for some become monotonous, or which may feel too connected to the Catholic Church for others — but rather, one may create one's own individual formula of prayer. Such a prayer has an unbelievable effect upon healing the body and upon raising the consciousness toward illumination.

QUESTION: How does meditation aid in helping the personality, or low self, attune with the Oversoul?

ANSWER: The low self is constituted of the physical, emotional and mental bodies. The physical body is composed of an objective physical body and an etheric double which interpenetrates it. This etheric, or vital, body supplies the lifeforce energizing the body. The physical form is dead without the presence of this etheric body. The heart seed atom is the principal focal point of the contact between these two bodies.

The emotional, or astral, body is composed of matter of the emotional astral plane. The emotional seed atom, located in the solar plexus, is the contact point between the physical and the astral bodies. The mental body has its contact point with the brain in the pineal gland. The lower mental body is the vehicle of concrete knowledge. The higher mental body is the vehicle of abstract ideas and ideals.

Meditation brings all three bodies under the control of the High Self. It disciplines and balances the bodies. It stimulates the mental seed atom in the brain to respond to the higher inspiration sent down by the Oversoul — the High Self. It aligns the three bodies with the Oversoul, which repolarizes them. It stabilizes the vibration of all three lower bodies and gradually imposes on them a higher rhythm. When the initiate makes contact with the High Self through meditation, and keys his or her bodies to the vibrations of the Oversoul, this one has found the "peace that passeth all understanding."

Chapter 6

Ancient Wisdom

QUESTION: Exactly what is the sutratma?

ANSWER: The sutratma is a delicate connecting link between the personality and the High Self. It is called the life thread, which becomes strong and radiant as the soul progresses. This thread soul is a fragment of the spiritual Self, passing like a thread through the five subtle bodies. It runs through successive generations, through all the personalities of earth.

It is the life ray upon which forces, like many beads, are hung. This life thread is vitalized with life energy sent down from the Oversoul and connected with the three centers of the physical nature in the cranium — the pineal gland, the pituitary body and the alta major center. The vital point on the head is the entrance of the sutratma into the center at the top of the head, through which the spirit body withdraws at the moment of death.

Karma is spoken of as an entangling thread. The individual existence is said to be like a rope stretching from the finite to the infinite, formed of immeasurable fine threads which are sometimes entangled and sometimes straight. Again it is said that every soul weaves its destiny, thread by thread, round itself from birth to death guided by the inner being, as a spider weaves its web.

The sutratma becomes the sushumna in the brain and continues down the spine to end in the root chakra. The sutratma is the silver cord which breaks at death, releasing the spirit into higher planes.

QUESTION: I have always puzzled over words written in a little booklet called *Light on the Path*. How do you interpret the meaning of these words:

"These rules are written for all disciples. Attend you to them. Before the eyes can see they must be incapable of tears. Before the ear can hear it must have lost its sensitiveness. Before the voice can speak in the presence of the Masters it must have lost the power to wound. Before the soul can stand in the presence of the Masters its feet must be washed in the blood of the heart."

ANSWER: First let me say the marvelous little book called *Light on the Path,* to which you refer, was written in 1932 by an "early pioneer" New Age mystic — Percilla Lawyer Randolph. However, the words you quote I do believe were written in a different publication, by a different author. I wish I could remember the book and the author, but I cannot.

These words describe the battle between the Higher Self and the lower self on the battleground of the emotional (astral) plane.

Eyes are windows of the soul.

To see with the inner vision one must have the light that illuminates the soul. To attain this vision the "window" must be clean. It must not be blurred nor clouded by tears of desire, wounded pride, annoyance and anxiety, or the things of Earth.

To be incapable of tears is to have faced and conquered the lower self and have an equilibrium which cannot be shaken by personal emotions. No grief, disappointment or fear can shake the personality loose from its fixed hold on the Higher Self, which inspires it. No pleasure or sensation can lure it away from its goal, from its fixed purpose. All vibrations of physical life have lost their tyranny. The initiate has found peace and his/her eyes are incapable of tears for earthly things — only tears for God.

Before the ear can hear, it must have lost its sensitiveness.

Ears are doors through which knowledge is gained. To have the ear lose its sensitiveness is to have your attention focussed on your goal, on your Higher Self, and be undisturbed by the vibrations that come from the lower self. It is to shut out all external sounds and to listen to the voice of the silence. It is to tune your ear to the vibrations of the Higher Self and "listen in" to the inner voice undisturbed. It is to listen to the call of the Holy Nahd, the celestial stream of love energy from the throne of God.

To speak is to communicate, and the Master represents the Higher Self. Therefore to speak in the presence of the Master is to be in communion with the Higher Self. Before this can be accomplished, the voice must have lost its power to wound. The seeker must have conquered the lower self. One must have worked through one's lower passions and emotions, including the tendency to judge self or others, before one's voice can be heard by one's Higher Self.

The power to wound comes from selfishness, the instinct of self-defense and self-preservation. To lose this power one must surrender one's worldly rights. You must never rise up in unrighteous condemnation or in judgment. You must be "like a little child" in order to be able to enter the Kingdom of God.

Again, to speak means to serve, and to serve must be not for glory or reward, but selfless. The highest type of service is possible only when the lower self is crucified and the Higher Self serves, not catering to the needs of humanity, externally, but becoming one with it. The High Self serves in accordance with the hierarchical plan, which may require service of an external nature or of an esoteric nature, or both.

Before you, the disciple, have mastered your lower self and silenced your emotions and can stand fearless, calm and self-possessed in the presence of your Master, or can center your whole consciousness in your Higher Self, you must have surrendered your heart, the seat of your emotions and desires. Your life must be consecrated to your Higher Self, to the Divine Spirit within.

QUESTION: The following words are used a lot in the Ancient Wisdom. Would you enlarge upon their general meaning?

1. Consecration
2. Imagination
3. Purification
4. Self-control
5. The Seven Bodies
6. Incarnation
7. Vibration
8. Alignment
9. Liberation of the soul
10. The Planes

ANSWER: 1. Consecration is the act of separation from a common cause to a sacred one. It is devoting one's self to a sacred purpose. Or to God. It is the subjugation of one's will to the will of Higher Intelligence. It is the working through of the lower self to reach the Higher Self — the Divine Spirit within.

2. Imagination is the creation of an image in the mind — a model of our desires. It is also the faculty directing the work of creation.

Will and imagination are the two principal qualities of the Oversoul. The will is the male power and is allied to the solar forces. Imagination is the female power and is linked with the lunar forces.

3. Purification means the process of attaining unmixed, unadulterated purity. Absolute purity would mean no thing, it would not act on the senses. There would be no action or reaction. No positive or negative polarization, simply neutral. It would mean absolute equality. In a more concrete sense of the word, when we speak of physical purity we mean clearing the system of all lower and coarse matter, of congestions, toxins, especially those that stimulate the senses and lower the vibration of the etheric body.

Emotional purity means having the heart center unattached to all mixed emotions, such as hatred, fear, anxiety, worry, suspicion, jealousy, anger, etc., and free from all sinister motives, so that the emotional body can reflect the Higher Self. The ideal state in this case would be when all the lower emotions are transmuted into love, then the emotional body is stilled and its vibrations are so refined that they have become synchronous with those of the Higher Self.

Mental purity, or purity of thought, would be an abstraction. By purifying the mind or our thoughts we would eliminate from our mind all thoughts of our lower selves and gradually still the mental body so that thoughts from abstract levels and from the intuitional planes can find a receptive sheet whereon they may enscribe themselves.

4. Self-control is the mastery of the self. It is the mastery of the lower self by the Higher Self — the impersonal Self. It is self-discipline — the discipline to regularly follow meditation, yoga or some other spiritual practice. It is bringing all these lower bodies under the control of the soul. It is aligning the

lower bodies with the Higher Self and holding them steady within its circumference. Self-control is the key to all higher developments on all planes.

The process of achieving self-control is not through either rigidity or self-righteousness. In other words, it does not mean behaving in a "holier than thou" fashion. Nor does it mean rigidly denying that you experience difficult emotions such as fear, anger, sadness, jealousy and so on. It means that you work to release your attachment to these emotions. You experience them, learn from them, express them in some positive way perhaps, and then release them to flow from you.

5. The seven bodies refers to the organization of the elements of which the bodies are composed and to the different aspects which are manifested in ourselves. We contain in ourselves every element found in the universe. Our three aspects are: the Monad, as pure Spirit, the Father/Mother in Heaven; the Ego, Higher Self, or Individuality; the Personality, or lower self, the physical plane person.

6. Incarnation is the assumption of a human body, and the nature and state of a human being in order to gain experience. It is a unit of divine life, seeking expression on the physical plane through the medium of form. Each human being is an incarnation of God, and no being can become a god without passing through the human cycles.

7. Vibration is the rhythmic movement of a body. The more dense the body is, the slower the vibration. The original vibration of matter was caused at the dawn of manifestation, by an impulse, by the combination of positive electrical units with negative electrical units. Our object should be to attune our personal vibration to the vibrations of the Higher Self, and to synchronize it later on with that of the Monad.

8. Alignment is the act of bringing the lower self under

the influence of the Higher Self, so that the Higher Self is the directing force, and is in communication, unobstructed and free from all interference, straight through, with the lower self.

9. Liberation is the act of releasing the Self — the soul — from the lower selves. It is freeing the indwelling life from the veils that hide, and from the sheaths that imprison. Liberation from karmic law is freedom — no more mortal incarnations.

10. Planes are states of spirit-matter, permeating one another. The solar system is divided into seven planes, each of which is subdivided into seven subplanes. The highest plane of the subplanes is called the atomic plane. Planes also contain "worlds" and "kingdoms."

QUESTION: I do not understand exactly what is meant by the expression "the Seven Rays?" What are they? What kind of energy do they express? How do they influence our lives?

ANSWER: The Seven Rays are the different aspects of force by means of which the Logos manifests Itself. The Cosmic Logos manifests through seven solar systems. Our Solar Logos manifests through seven sacred planets, and the seven planetary Logoi express themselves through seven types of humans, which receive the seven types of force through seven centers in their bodies.

These seven forces or seven streams of energy are called Seven Rays, three of which are called Rays of Aspect and the remaining four, Rays of Attributes. These rays are as follows:

Rays of Aspect
1. The ray of will or power, expressing dynamic energy;

2. The ray of love-wisdom, expressing attractive energy;
3. The ray of activity or adaptability, expressing pranic energy.

Rays of Attribute
4. The ray of harmony and rhythm, expressing Buddhic energy;
5. The ray of concrete knowledge or science, expressing neutral energy;
6. The ray of abstract idealism or devotion, expressing emotional energy;
7. The ray of ceremonial law, expressing negative energy, devotion.

For those who seek to become initiates, it is essential they should know what their dominant ray is. This will guide them toward their mission in serving humanity. It is also important to determine the rays of those whom they wish to help or teach, so that they can approach them accordingly.

Although each person possesses a dominant ray, he or she also reveals all the other rays in a more or less different degree and may, by wise effort, integrate his or her dominant ray with all seven of the rays.

The ray of the High Self is constant, but the personality ray varies from life to life. It may or may not correspond to the High Self ray.

A soul who is on the First Ray is an aggressive type of soul, one who has its fixed opinions, one who is a powerful leader, like Napoleon, Caesar or Blavatsky. Will power drives a soul of this type to perfection by using dynamic will power in purifying the lower vehicles and in the higher service of humanity.

A soul of the Second Ray is of a sympathetic nature, its path of least resistance lies along the line of expansion. This soul will realize oneness with all services of love. It is a master of compassion, like Christ, and a master of wisdom, like Buddha, or a master of unselfish leadership, like Moses.

A Third Ray soul represents activity and adaptability. It is a soul who knows the systematic adaptation of all knowledge, of all means to the end in view, and the accumulation of needed material for helping the world.

A soul of the Fourth Ray is temperamentally artistic. It reaches perfection through the method of inner realization of beauty and harmony.

A Fifth Ray soul is the scientific soul who applies its concrete mind to some problems for helping humanity. This soul gathers information on the forces of nature and should utilize them for the service of humankind.

A Sixth Ray soul is one of devotion and sacrifice. It endeavors to perfect itself through the love of some individual or an ideal, like the saints and the Christian mystics.

A soul of the last and Seventh Ray reaches liberation through understanding and intelligent application of the law to its life and to the service of its fellow beings.

QUESTION: You teach often of the various "planes." But exactly what is a spiritual plane and how many are there?

ANSWER: Planes are states of spirit-matter, permeating one another. Another way to explain it is that a plane is a certain range or extent of consciousness.

From the threefold Supreme Being, or Godhead — which is called the Father, Son and Holy Ghost — proceed the Seven

Spirits before the Throne of God, forming the first cosmic plane. These Logoi contain within themselves all the great divine hierarchies. According to Ancient Wisdom, there are 49 hierarchies on the second cosmic plane, 343 on the third, etc. Each of those is also divided and subdivided (by septencey divisions) so that in the lowest cosmic plane, where the solar systems manifest, the number of divisions and subdivisions is almost infinite.

The seventh, or lowest, cosmic plane represents our solar system, as well as other solar systems in the universe.

Our Solar Logos expresses Him/Herself through the sacred planets, which are His/Her seven energy centers.

Our solar system is also divided into seven planes. Each of these planes is again divided into seven subplanes. The highest subplane in each plane is called "atomic," because its atoms cannot be further subdivided without passing from that plane to the one above it.

The seven planes of our nature are: Physical; Astral; Mental; Buddhic; Nirvanic; Paranirvanic; Celestial.

The seven subdivisions of the lowest (physical) plane are: solid; liquid; gaseous; etheric; super-etheric; sub-atomic; atomic.

The four lower subplanes of the Mental plane constitute the mental body (Rupa) and the three higher subplanes the causal body (Arupa).

From the point of view of humans there are seven types or planes of consciousness. These are: mineral consciousness; vegetable consciousness; animal consciousness; human consciousness; spiritual consciousness; atomic consciousness; God consciousness.

The teachers of the hierarchy state that cosmic consciousness is on seven planes of which three are inconceivable and four are cognizable by the highest adepts. The lowest four are: terrestrial consciousness; astral consciousness; lower psychic consciousness; higher psychic consciousness.

The above planes of consciousness are also divided and subdivided into infinite numbers of subplanes.

QUESTION: In your Wisdom Teachings you have mentioned the Law of Economy, the Law of Attraction, and the Law of Synthesis. Can you enlighten us further about these Laws?

ANSWER: Law is a codified system of limitations. These limitations are the creations of the innate mind and belong to form. The lower the mind or the consciousness, the more the limitations. The higher the consciousness, the less the limitations. When consciousness becomes absolute, form and limitations disappear.

When spirit manifests itself in the lowest or densest form of matter, the laws or limitations governing these substances are the most exact. There is absolutely no choice. The laws of gravitation and cohesion, the laws of one, two or three dimensional worlds, the laws of time and space must be obeyed. When the dense bodies become liquid or gas, they no longer obey all the same laws and we, for want of better terms, state that a "higher" law is in operation. When the manifestation extends into the vegetable and animal kingdoms, the law loses its value. In the human kingdom, choice, or the will of the soul, decides what action to take.

Humankind in its infancy needed and needs more laws — restrictions — than in its maturity. The unrighteous are under moral laws, but the righteous need no formulations of laws since they have risen above the temptation level. An average soul must work under natural laws. An adept, by full knowledge of them, can transcend these laws and perform "miracles" by the intelligent use of his or her will, in obedience to "higher" laws.

When perfection is attained and oneness is accomplished, all laws and limitations disappear and the soul becomes liberated.

The Law of Economy is the first law governing manifestation. It controls the unfoldment of the third aspect of the divine life — the objective manifestation, that of matter. It is the law which adjusts all that concerns the material evolution of the cosmos to the best possible advantage, and with the least expenditure of force. It causes matter to follow the line of least resistance.

According to this law, there is no waste in nature. Every atom is placed in its right place to perform certain functions. Atoms are grouped together to aid each other in performance of a plan. After this function is performed, and there is no more need of it, the organ performing that function disintegrates and the atoms are used somewhere else.

It is according to this law that atoms are distributed in a form in the most economical way. The beautiful geometrical forms of crystals, the honeycomb, and the arrangement of cells in living organisms are manifestations of this law. The vegetable and animal cells generally tend to take a 14-sided figure — a tetrakaidecahedron — in order to fill the space compactly.

It is according to this law that atoms are perfected, and the evolution of the human race is carried on. Reincarnation is due to this law. It is desire that causes rebirth, attracting us back to earth life again. Liberation comes when desirelessness is attained.

The Law of Attraction is the second law governing manifestation. It controls the unfoldment of the second aspect of the divine life — that of love-wisdom. It is according to this law that our solar system is held revolving around the Sirian system; that our planets revolve around our sun; that atoms and molecules revolve around a center; that all chemical actions, cohesion, precipitation, crystallization, and so on, are brought about. According to this law, matter is utilized in form building, and in the adaptation of form to the need. After form reaches its culmination it is destroyed by the Law of Repulsion.

It is according to the Law of Attraction that we make contact with the external world. The Law of Economy governs the material process with which we are not so much consciously concerned; the Law of Attraction governs our connection with other units and groups. It is this Law — the Law of Attraction and Repulsion — that produces cyclic and periodic effects both in nature and in humans.

The Law of Synthesis is the third law governing manifestation and controls the unfoldment of the first aspect of the divine life — divine will and power. It is the law governing the fact that all things, abstract and concrete, exist as one. It is this law that governs the thoughtform of that One of the Cosmic Logoi, in whose consciousness both our system and the greater center have a part.

This law comes into play after Spirit and matter have blended and adapted themselves to each other; after the concrete and the abstract have become one; after spiritual liberation is attained and after the form is destroyed through the withdrawal of Spirit. The Law of Economy no longer functions. It is transcended. The Law of Attraction has fallen away, and the Law of Synthesis is now the primary law of the heavenly being.

QUESTION: Is suffering connected to karma? Otherwise, what is the purpose of suffering and pain?

ANSWER: According to Ancient Wisdom, pleasure and pain are necessary phases in the process of evolution. Pain is a sensory reaction caused by resistance to the course of the ever-flowing stream of earth life — in matter. Often that which one thinks brings pleasure is the cause of pain — such as a hangover following excessive drinking. If there were no resistance there would be no awareness to external things. Pain therefore brings us in touch with the external world, with the not-Self. It causes us to look to a Higher Source for healing, for understanding what we might have done to cause pain, and what we can do to escape it. It awakens us to Self-realization.

The second object of suffering is the adaptation of form to the need, the perfecting of form and of our vehicles. Through pain we make effort and exert our energies and this strengthens our vehicles and our character.

The third reason is purification of that for which form is a temporary vehicle. Pain is sometimes involved in breaking up the form when the form is outgrown, according to the soul's karmic pattern. It is often a painful process to uproot our desire nature and turn the tendency of our life stream to the opposite direction.

Fourth, pain is a great teacher. We would keep on violating nature's laws until we destroyed ourselves, were it not for the warning of this wise teacher.

Fifth, pain gives us power, when properly interpreted. "Power is pain transmuted." It gives us power of character. "It is a royal thing to suffer and say nothing about it," said Marcus Aurelius.

All humanity is striving for happiness. Complete happiness is a state of consciousness which comes when all our vehicles are in harmony, when their vibrations are rhythmic and in tune with each other, when we can give full expression to our emotions and ideas without any hindrance or resistance.

This is a glorious thing to have, but we cannot have it until our vehicles are purified — which often requires karmic suffering. So we should strive not for happiness, but for joy. Joy is becoming. It is a state of consciousness which comes to us, not when we are having pleasures of the three worlds, but when we see clearly through sorrow. Because in that sorrow we see the Great Plan, through our tears we see the eternal goal. When we are in sorrow we often gain spiritual perception.

Suffering is a quality of form, of self. To overcome suffering is to become selfless, desireless. In other words it is to follow the path of acceptance, renunciation, surrender, submission, non-resistance. It is simply a change of attitude on our part. Instead of going against the will of God, it is giving up the desire for earthly "things" and desire, instead, the "things" of the spirit.

"Give to him that asketh thee, and from him that would borrow of thee turn not thou away." (Mt. 3:42) "Be not overcome of evil; but overcome evil with good." (Rom. 12:21) "...whosoever shall smite thee on thy right cheek, turn to him the other also.... And whosoever shall compel thee to go a mile, go with him twain." (Mt. 5:39,41) But go, not with resentment, but willingly, joyously.

If karma has placed you in hard circumstances, overcome them by serving others, by purifying the heart seed atom. If you find that your plans to help have failed, do not feel disappointed, but instead feel sincerely that your help was not wanted. If your loved ones forsake you or are separated from you, allow yourself to grieve and then transmute your grief to selfless love, impersonal love, the love of One that includes all. And you will feel, you will know, that there is no separation. This is the path that leads you to peace with understanding.

In other words, we are told to be positive — non-resistant to all below us but negative to all above us. The struggle is not for things of this world, but for the spiritual life.

QUESTION: Would you please say something about the substance you call Azoth or Akasha?

ANSWER: The whole universe — and by that I mean the *infinite* universe, whose limitless reaches we cannot encompass in our finite minds, *is filled with One substance.* Even science has conceded that the 93 elements which they have succeeded in segregating, one from the other, have a common derivative in *One* substance — an infinite ever-expanding universe of substance which is acted upon by *Divine Mind,* that force which we designate as God or the God Principle. These mental impingements of thoughtforce upon the ethers (universal substance) bring forth, through natural chemical action and reaction (we call it vibration), millions upon millions of different forms — yet, and here is the great fact, *basically they are one and the same.*

For, since God, or the Creator, has sent creative thought to act chemically upon this substance, filling all space, we can readily see that *all* things in the universe are *One* in essence. And we, as human individuals have, as the Master taught, derived our lives, our eternal spirits and our physical bodies from a substance which is universal and common to all. *This* is the true Fatherhood-Motherhood of God, and the Brotherhood-Sisterhood of humanity.

Jesus said, "In the image and likeness of God are ye created," meaning not the physical form which must, in the course of inevitable dissolution, return to its original substance; but rather the potential powers and possibilities of that One substance, *the body of God*, which is within all, through all, and of all. Yet the body of God is not divisible into a million or so tiny bits, one for each of us. Rather it is indivisible, inseparable in its power; for even as a tiny drop of ocean water contains within itself all the minerals, powers and potentialities of the entire ocean, its source — so this God substance within us, *our source*, contains within itself, all the attributes of the *whole God substance,* from which it came.

And further, it *must* be the cohesive principle holding all forms of life together; forever flowing through each individual link in the endless chain of every form of life. With this thought in mind, examine each separate teaching of the Master Teachers. You will find this universal Oneness to be the basic principle upon which every tenet is formed. It is the simplified *why*. In Ancient Wisdom, the Substance was called Azoth and Akasha.

Thus we see *why* Jesus said we must love, universally, all forms of life, be it bird, beast, creeping thing or humankind. Comprehending this fact brings new meaning to the words, "Ye are Gods in the making." For God, Divine Mind, Divine Substance, *is* around, about and through *all* things *for God is all things to all* souls — the indwelling life *in* all things and *life is supremely One!*

QUESTION: What exactly is meant by the divine androgynous? — being both male-female in one?

ANSWER: The brain is covered by what is called the cerebral cortex. A cortex is the bark, or surface layer, of an organ. The cerebral cortex thus becomes the external gray layer of the brain

— the crust of the Holy Mountain. This cerebral cortex, or crust of the brain, is penetrated by a substance called pia mater which medical science calls the vascular membrane of the brain. It is also called, even by medical science, "kind or tender mother," pia meaning Godly, tender, protecting, nourishing — while mater means mother. Thus the crust of the brain embraces the pia mater, or the mother substance.

The pia mater, or the mother of the cerebrum, in turn contains in her embrace an embryo of the divine hermaphrodite. This Celestial Child is called by many names;
1. the divine hermaphrodite;
2. the divine androgynous;
3. the Christ-Child;
4. the Christ in the human being;
5. the celestial twins.

This Celestial Child contains both male and female attributes.

Even though we appear in our flesh bodies as either one gender or the other, the spirit which is made in the image and likeness of God is neither male nor female but is both: androgynous, we call it. The male form even now reflects many feminine qualities, while the female form reflects many masculine. In the male, the masculine qualities dominate. In the female, the feminine. Ancient Wisdom does not teach that we must unite with some lost soul mate to gain our complete oneness with Perfection, but that we must develop within ourselves whatever remains dormant in our natures, to become whole, to develop gradually — over a span of millenniums — into divine hermaphrodites, male and female in one. This may not mean actual physical change, but rather that we should strive to integrate and equally value both male and female aspects of our natures, both strength and gentleness, for example.

Ancient Wisdom

Concerning birth and rebirth, Ancient Wisdom teaches how the image of the incoming ego is implanted, through the mechanism of the mental reflecting ether, in the sperm of the father. The sperm of the father, planted in the ovum of the mother, transfers the image of the incoming ego. Having received the image unto itself, the ovum in the uterus of the mother sets into action the operations necessary to produce a physical form in which to house the incoming ego. The sperm of the father in this case reflects the image of the incoming ego.

The brain is a reproduction of the sperm. Just as the sperm has coiled within it an egoic image, so does the brain hold within itself an image of the future you. The brain, including the spinal cord, is only a larger spermatozoon containing an egoic image of what you will be in the future. This brain spermatozoon holds within itself in embryonic form the Divinity within you, or the undeveloped godlike form in embryo within yourself.

This embryonic godform within you lies in sleeping repose until such time as it is given birth through your own spiritual evolvement and endeavors.

The kundalini rises up the spine and spends its power in the cells of the brain. Like the ovum swallowing up the sperm-germ, kundalini swallows up the sperm-germ of the Christ-embryo in the brain. The brain then becomes a uterus, housing the embryonic Godspark within, impregnated with lifeforce. This embryo cannot come into birth, however, without the power of the Holy Breath, the Word.

QUESTION: Who conceived the signs of the zodiac?

ANSWER: We know the Egyptians understood the orbit of the Earth around the sun. They knew the Earth's size, how to calculate time and were familiar with cosmic knowledge. While the Greeks accepted credit for such teachings, every Greek philosopher except Aristotle studied in Egypt. The Greeks were only reporters. So without a doubt, the priests and Ptahs of the Egyptian Mystery Schools conceived the signs of the zodiac. And they were given the information by the Builders of the pyramids — who, again, were, I believe, extraterrestrials.

Every culture includes the signs of the zodiac. The Mayans had 16. The Chaldeans had 6. Today we have 12. Every sign is drawn behind the ecliptic — the path of Earth around the sun. The original purpose of the signs of the zodiac was to mark the movement of the Earth around the sun. Someone thousands of years ago had to know about the ecliptic, had to understand gravitational astronomy. Who else but space travelers? There is no way to grasp the signs of the zodiac without understanding gravitational astronomy.

The Earth precesses through the signs of the zodiac, moving slowly along the ecliptic. The plane of the axis of the Earth as it wobbles, moves through every sign of the zodiac very slowly — requiring 25,856.25 years to complete the cycle. We call it 26,000 to be general.

The sum of the base diagonal of the Great Pyramid adds up to 25,856.25 inches — exactly the number of years in a precessional cycle. It is mathematically perfect. Its Builders knew the science of building to cosmic measurements. They used cosmic computers.

The Great Pyramid is symbolic of what life and death and initiation are about. It was never meant to be used as a tomb.

QUESTION: I am occasionally asked "What is initiation?" I understand what it means, but I can't explain it in a few words that others will understand. Can you explain it in terms that will be meaningful to others?

ANSWER: Initiation means the beginning of an awakening. It means the soul is entering the spiritual life. With your first initiation you are taking the first step into the spiritual kingdom. Just as the Monadic force of your being passed from the Universal Kingdom of Monads into the vegetable, and from the vegetable to the animal, and from the animal kingdom into the human kingdom, so you now pass from the human kingdom into the spiritual kingdom, into the university of the Supreme Intelligence — the Hall of Wisdom.

Initiation takes place after you have learned many lessons of life during a number of incarnations in human form. Only then are you ready for initiation. All souls will eventually enter the path of initiation, but it often requires many incarnations to prepare the soul for this step. But the process can be hastened. You can earn your own salvation slowly, or take the Kingdom of God by "storm" in the course of a few incarnations by learning the lessons of Earth life rapidly, and passing on from class to class.

There are two ways of learning. The slow method is by experience — by identifying yourself with matter and experiencing all the vibrations, enjoying all the pleasures life gives you, all the sorrow, all the suffering, and finding out in the end that "all is vanity and vexation of the soul."

The second is by strenuous thinking and living, by learning from the experience of others, by purifying your lower self and transmuting all the coarse vibrations into those more harmonious. By unfolding your consciousness, by realizing the unity of all selves, by seeking the light, by expanding your vision into God's plans for the world and consciously cooperating with the Mother/Father God to further these plans through prayer, service and study.

Each initiation marks the passing of the soul into a higher class. Each initiation is a further awakening of consciousness. It is the transition from one point of polarization to another. It is a progressive at-one-ment of our lower personality with the Higher Self, your Oversoul; with your self and all selves; between your Higher Self and the Universal Self; by removing the veils, the barriers between them.

It is the widening of your vision from initiation to initiation until you embrace the whole universe. You are liberated from the Wheel of Birth-Death and need no more return to the world of matter.

QUESTION: How can the Infinite be explained so that the finite mind can understand it?

ANSWER: The scope of our consciousness is limited, and with its finite properties it cannot measure the Infinite. Its limitations prevent a true judgment of the Infinite and its omnipotence. The limited mental substance of our present consciousness cannot conceive of the wealth, the riches, the substance, the being, the qualities of the Infinite, the Supreme, any more than an animal can understand the equations of geometry. The finite cannot understand God's geometrizing. Humanity can only base its reasoning and its logic upon the scope of the individual's experience in the finite world of physical nature. One cannot judge the Supreme and Grand Architect by the sidereal kingdom within one's observation.

Scientists can understand an aggregate of infinitesimals such as the electrons, atoms, molecules and cells upon which our physical form is built; but the scientists cannot explain the law of action these infinitesimals assume in expressing as a physical form; nor do they understand how the lifeforce operates within the cells of the human form. Little wonder, then, that they cannot understand the process of the law which operates the human superphysical being — the mind movements and the properties of the soul. Science cannot accept the proposition that the true part of humans — the soul — surpasses the elements or constituents of which the physical form is composed, and can even operate outside the limitations of that form.

It is this inner Infinite which has built and which supports and directs the form it inhabits. Since the physical figure is only a shadow of the inner Infinite, it follows that the finite form can never be completely understood unless a knowledge of that which is hidden within and behind it is first understood. Regardless of the scope of our finite knowledge, it can never be complete until it includes an understanding of the inner Infinite.

A law which applies to the physical plane does not apply to the metaphysical plane. A law which applies to the realms of time and space cannot be applied to that which is indivisible. Intellect guides the form while intuition is the voice of the inner Infinite. Intellect — truth filled with intellectual reasoning — seldom hears the subtle soundings of intuition. Intuition does not reason, does not need logic, but the law of intuition is as definite as the law of electricity when operating through its proper channels. It only remains for the finite operations of humankind to plug into the reservoir of the higher mind to draw upon wisdom and intuition. The reasoning and the logic found within the spiritual reservoir are based upon wisdom, not a finite knowledge.

Our finite reasoning relegates magic to the realm of the finite. Yet magic is the logic of the infinite. Intuition comprehends the vast and complex operations of the infinite, while intellect only comprehends the scope of its personal experiences.

Intellect is that which observes the actions of another; intuition is that which reveals the causes of his/her actions. Intellect is based upon an accumulation of unreliable knowledge; intuition is based upon an awareness of spiritual laws without reference to data. Reason operating with restricted vision establishes a set of rules based upon ignorance or a meager knowledge; intuition bases its set of rules upon full vision and a knowledge of the laws of cause and effect, and how that law adapts itself to differing sets of circumstances. To finite logic, this higher reasoning would seem to have no standard. A child cannot understand the force of electricity. Humanity cannot understand the higher forces of Akasha, Azoth or the Divine Substance.

It is not enough to say Om Tat Sat (I am That), unless we realize that everyone else is also That, according to the scope of his/her understanding. "You are Brahman," a guru instructed one of his disciples. So the inflated neophyte planted himself in the middle of a narrow elephant path. "Get out of the way," said the elephant driver of an oncoming elephant. The disciple did not budge. "Step aside," cried the elephant driver. Still the disciple held his place. The elephant, without hesitation, lifted the disciple with his trunk and placed him to the side of the path.

"What happened?" asked the disciple of his Master. "If I am Brahman, why did not the elephant recognize it?" "Indeed you are Brahman," said the Master, "but why did you not heed the warning of the driver who is also Brahman and step out of the path of the elephant Brahman?" We cannot believe that God only exists for us: God exists for all, and all are a part of the Divine.

QUESTION: What is the mystical meaning of the lotus?

ANSWER: The lotus flower belongs to the water lily family. It is not the lotus of the botanists, which is genus of the pea family. The Egyptian lotus (castilia) was a water lily (Nymphaea lotus). So also was the sacred lotus of the Hindus. The lotus fruits of the Greeks were used for making bread. When Odysseus reached the country of the lotus-eaters, (Lotophagi) many of his sailors, after eating the lotus, lost all will to return home. Both Greeks and Romans used the expression "to eat the lotus" to denote forgetfulness.

The lotus is used as a symbol of the soul and of the cosmos, and the indissoluble union between the soul and the universe. The lotus symbolized the Hindu Trinity (Trinumuti) Brahma (creator), Vishnu (preserver) and Siva (destroyer). The well known mantra OM MANI PADME HUM means "I am the jewel in the Lotus," which signifies "Oh my God within me," for the lotus is the universal symbol of cosmos, abstract and concrete, as the absolute totality and the jewel is the spiritual soul or God.

The lotus plant grows up through the water, having its roots in the mud and spreading its flowers in the air above. This typifies the soul. The root in the mud represents the physical life and the personality. The stalk passing up through the water typifies the link to the Oversoul and the flower floating on the water and opening to the sky is emblematic of the higher mind and the spiritual Oversoul.

The seeds of the lotus, even before they generate, contain perfectly formed leaves, the miniature shapes of what they will become one day as perfected plants — just as the acorn contains the image of the future oak. This is a beautiful picture of the soul whose form is evolved from the inner toward the outer and whose external shape assumes gradually the form of the model within itself — the jewel — the spirit.

The lotus also symbolizes generation, growing in water which is the feminine symbol, and responding to the heat or fire of the sun, which is the masculine principle. Vishnu was represented with a lotus growing out of his navel on the universe of Brahma, evolving out of the central point.

The lotus was held sacred not only by the Hindus and the Egyptians, but also by the Christian churches of the Romans. In every early picture of the Annunciation the archangel Gabriel appeared to the Virgin Mary holding in his hand a spray of water lilies, which replace the lotus, and typify fire and water. So the lotus universally symbolizes the underlying idea in all religions that is the emanation of the objective from the subjective divine ideation passing from the abstract into the concrete or visible form.

In mysticism, the different astral centers, or the organs to behold superphysical things, are called "wheels" (chakras) or "lotus flowers," having different numbers of petals. As the soul unfolds these organs, these petals also are developed. In modern Mystery Schools the lotus symbolizes the God-realized liberated soul totally joined to its Oversoul.

QUESTION: I always wondered why some races of people have darker skins than others, and how there must be some kind of mystery behind God's reasons for having it the way it is. I would love to know more about a topic such as this.

ANSWER: Why are there races, why are there different colors of skin? What was the purpose? Why did God do this? Why indeed was the Tower of Babel that caused there to be different languages between us?

Let's go back in time and see the human lifewave chosen to evolve on this particular planet. And let's try to tune into the evolutionary process taking place at that time, and see God's purpose in "creating" the yellow race, the black race, the brown race, the white race, the red race.

Our physical manifestations have obviously changed somewhat in the past 18 million years since the Planetary Logos first incarnated in a physical body. Many things influenced racial differences, from climate and food supply, to social and cultural conflict, to intermarriage between the races.

When the present lifewave of souls inhabiting Earth first incarnated into Earth bodies, we were allowed to choose the race into which we would incarnate. Then, with proceeding incarnations, it became not a matter of choice — it was a matter of which race would enable us to experience the "training" the soul needed at the time of rebirth.

Let's say John Smith was ready to incarnate on Earth and his information at the planetary gateway through which his soul was arriving indicated that his soul's growth would be most benefitted by a black physical manifestation. This means the Lords of Karma would send him into the black race because his soul needed experience in that race. Every single one of us have, or will have manifested in every one of our races, wearing the color of that race.

This was done so that the soul of each of us could gain experience in the different cultures, the different thoughts, the different feelings, the different emotions, the different religions, the different philosophies of each of Earth's races. So, I have manifested in the yellow race of China, in the black race of Africa, the brown race of India or South America, as an Indian in North America, and now I'm experiencing the white race. No race is superior to any other — all races contain older souls, souls that have experienced more incarnations. Each of us has to experience the soul development each particular race offers the soul.

At some time in the past you were in the dark skin of the black race, the white skin probably more than once, the yellow skin of China — we all certainly have come out of Egypt. But each incarnation offered certain soul development. This is why some find themselves in the dark skin. They are experiencing what that race has to offer them for this development and evolvement of their soul as only that particular race can give them.

There are different races and cultures because a very large part of our soul development for each person on this Earth involves learning to value difference, rather than to fear and seek power over those who are different. In order to learn to let go of intolerance, prejudice and judgement, we must learn to deal with difference. Therefore, difference had to be made manifest.

QUESTION: At your Ceremony of Initiation, held every Memorial Day Weekend, you were giving out scarabs, as well as crystals. Do scarabs have the same energy as crystals?

ANSWER: All the scarabs we've ever used at the Fire Initiation came from Egypt. They are placed under my personal pyramid here in California, in our prayer shrine. They are the symbol of eternal life. They possess a different type of vibratory current than the crystal, but their current is tremendously effective and powerful, especially when used during meditation. Also, these scarabs have absorbed vibrations from my pyramid, which gives you and I a timeless connection, wherever I might be.

In Egypt, these scarabs are also linked to the Great Pyramid in a very special way. The same "jinn" entities that operate under a certain magical formula to protect the pyramid, also work with these scarabs to charge and attune them in positive and divine ways with the lifeforce of the Great Pyramid. So everyone that has taken a scarab during the Fire Initiation is linked to the Great Pyramid in a most remarkable way.

QUESTION: In your writings you tell about the First Initiation. As you are my teacher, how can I arrange to have you bestow Shaktipat upon me so I can receive the complete and full initiation?

ANSWER: At our organization headquarters, once a year we present what we call the Fire Initiation. The Fire Initiation is one way to receive Shaktipat. Shaktipat is a word which means the transfer of energy from a teacher to a disciple for the purpose of stimulating the kundalini power which rests in the root chakra at the base of the spine.

Shaktipat at the Fire Initiation occurs after the sign of the cross is placed upon the forehead of the disciple by the teacher. Your kundalini power has been awakened and it's so powerful you may have visions and various different sensations occurring. Once the kundalini is awakened, you're never the same — you're transfigured and transformed.

It has to be a touch, either etherically, or there at the Fire Ceremony, or through some other initiatory ceremony. At our particular Fire Ceremony, the leader is absorbing power from higher dimensions, touching the forehead of the disciple in the sign of a cross during the ceremony, and the Shaktipat energy is transferred. The kundalini power within has been awakened. Continue to ask, to meditate and pray for the power of Shaktipat and unseen forces will eventually baptize you in initiation. Since you have requested my assistance, I shall pray to be among the unseen forces in my etheric form.

QUESTION: Under hypnotic regression could one recall the secret knowledge taught in the ancient Mystery Schools to an initiate?

ANSWER: Yes, indeed — depending upon how much of the secret knowledge one gained in a prelife. Few ever finished the seventh initiation.

QUESTION: What are the differences between metaphysical, applied and esoteric psychology?

ANSWER: Modern metaphysical psychology is the study of the our soul on the physical, astral and mental planes. It is the study of the laws of our mind in the objective, subjective or subconscious and the superconscious states, and of our waking, dreaming and sleeping consciousness. It is the search for the laws of thought transference, telepathy, premonitions, dreams, visions, etc. Applied psychology deals with the laws of the hidden powers of our subjective mind, and endeavors to find ways and means for developing these powers for our material prosperity and spiritual unfoldment.

Esoteric occult psychology is the study of the growth of our soul, the High Self and of the means of attaining at-one-ment of the personality with the soul, or the Divine Spirit. It is the study of the unfoldment of our consciousness through knowledge, which deals with the Self and the wisdom of the Oversoul and the Third Eye.

Chapter 7

Holy Nahd

QUESTION: You have said the mind is the soul's worst enemy — can you please explain?

ANSWER: The mind is a lower aspect of the soul. The soul is pure, while the mind aspect is contaminated by the impressions of the world, and by desires which cause an unending chain of reactions, enmeshing the soul in a web of karma.

The higher aspects of the soul continually seek to return to the home from which they came in the divine regions, but the mind, turned outward, constantly engulfs the soul in perpetual yearnings for earthly pleasures, wealth, passions, greed, self-aggrandizement, and attachments. It is this enmeshment which causes the soul to come again and again into birth in the world of matter. The soul and the mind are bound together, the soul following the mind into rebirth. The soul thus becomes a captive of the mind, which may run rampant, creating dire consequences.

Discovering the truth of this existing condition, the disciple seeks ever to overcome the outgoing tendencies of the mind by turning it inward, the better to seek dominance by the soul. This is the purpose of attunement with the Holy Nahd, the Audible Life Stream. The mind attuned to this Divine Sound experiences such an ecstatic awakening that it pauses in its outward seeking and, of itself, joyously turns inward to seek again and again the supreme contact. It is only through contact with the Sound Current that the soul attains permanent release from the prison wheel of rebirths.

The human form can be compared to a house with ten doors. Nine of the ten doors, represented by the organs, open outward to the world and all of its temptations and conditions. There is only one door — the tenth — which leads us to the inner realm, the doorway to our true home. That doorway is through the Brahmarandra, or the Third Eye chakra.

Karma binds us to the world, and perpetual desires create continuing karma. The teachings of the Masters proclaim that the road to liberation from these fetters is through turning within and attuning to the Holy Nahd, the Divine Sound Current. Through such an attunement we can find permanent peace, which leads to the only existing happiness on the plane of Earth.

It is our egotism, passions, and desire for earthly possessions that creates within us attachment for the Earth which draws the soul into incarnation again and again. Egotism causes us to lay claim to things, even our own bodies, and such attachments can completely occupy our minds. We can become so attached to our bodies that in the realms of the afterlife we automatically yearn to possess another human body, and that subconscious desire draws us again Earthward.

Liberation comes as we turn within, knock at the door of the Third Eye, and eventually enter into the White Light of Holy Nahd. It is through the White Light that karma can be destroyed. Once the mind, turning inward, experiences even a shadow of the bliss of Nahd, much of its racing madness after earthly pleasures vanishes. It has found the only source of delight capable of overpowering its desire for earthly things and passions.

QUESTION: You have taught much about attuning to the sound of the Holy Nahd, heard in the deep consciousness when one is able, through meditation, to hear it. Please explain the importance of hearing it, and its influence on the soul and the soul's spiritual evolution.

ANSWER: True mysticism and the science of the Sound Current usually appeal only to those souls who have never found real happiness with this world, who feel an attunement to something unseen.

This is not always true, however. There are many souls who have never been happy here in this world, but who have no desire to listen to the Sound Current. And certainly, there are people who have found happiness and also value a life of seeking and spiritual growth who have never even heard of the Sound Current.

Those who seek profound truth form a special class by themselves. These seekers, even though they may be surrounded by all the blessings and comforts of this world, will always know there is something of higher importance to strive for. These souls differ completely from the worldly souls who, desiring the pleasures of the world, feel miserable and unhappy when such pleasures are not realized.

True seekers do not turn only to the teachings of the Scriptures. However one may revere the Holy Bible, or the Vedas, or the Koran, the Upanishads, or any mystical writings, these seekers are aware that these books are divine teachings interpreted and written down by men in certain times and cultures, thus limited in perception and interpretation. They may revere such Scriptures, but they seek true knowledge through the Voice of the Sound Current. This is the "Comforter" which reveals all things to the true mystic.

While the Scriptures can only be interpreted according to one's limited understanding, such is not true of the teachings learned through the Sound Current. In meditations or prayer one meets the form of one's angel guardian and hears his or her voice speak, and the teachings gained through the "still small voice" are the true teachings, needing no individualized interpretation.

The soul is associated with various adversaries, both in its inner life and its outer involvements. Internally the soul is enmeshed in a web of human emotions — love, hate, anger, fear, greed, vanity, passion, jealousy. Externally it is involved in attachments to mother, father, brother, sister, husband, wife, children, friends, wealth, and all the pleasures of the senses. And the soul will not relinquish such involvements unless it is presented with a more enchanting substitute.

One such substitution is the Sound of the Holy Nahd. Union with such a Current brings such ecstatic rapture that the soul, once immersed in it, is willing to forego all pleasures of Earth to seek after it, because it is truly a connection with the Divine.

We experience illnesses of the body and traumatic response to the world in proportion to our attachment to the world and the things thereof. It is through meditation and repetition of the cosmic mantra, and devotion to the practice of Holy Nahd that we so increase our love for the Real and the Eternal, that we can begin to transcend our attachments to that which is impermanent.

QUESTION: In seeking to reach the Holy Nahd, is it possible to hear lesser voices and be led astray by misguiding entities and factors?

ANSWER: Truth is within. However, should one pause in one's seeking to become enamored with lower psychic powers, it then becomes possible for misguiding factors to disguise themselves and lead the disciple astray.

But when the disciple persists in repeating the cosmic mantra and fastening attention on the Third Eye, this is seeking development through the higher faculties. It is seeking through your own will and not relinquishing that will to another. Harm cannot befall the disciple who constantly calls the name of the Lord, or the cosmic mantra, or some other holy name, during the time of meditation, and who centers their attention in the Third Eye.

Problems develop only when one concentrates upon the lower chakras, or devotes unwise attention to things such as the ouija board and automatic writing. These avenues of psychic approach are acceptable only if one does not become enamored or controlled by them.

QUESTION: Speak more of detachment. Is there a "method" for achieving it, or does one simply have to struggle to "let go?"

ANSWER: Detachment comes automatically when one is devoted to Holy Nahd. Once Nahd is contacted, the mind is so enthralled that it is no longer tempted by worldly pleasures. It experiences "conversion," which means "to change from one use, function, or purpose, to another; transformation." Such conversion can be instantaneous, as was Paul's on his journey to Damascus.

Detachment means "to be in the world but not of it." Detachment means to strive, once one experiences even the first step of initiation, to create no more new karma and to disentangle the soul from the web already created. It does not mean to turn away from the world and all those that are loved —but to live so that all karmic ties are only ties of love.

QUESTION: Is it possible to hear the Sound Current even when one is not in meditation?

ANSWER: It most assuredly is. It is important for the disciple to gradually form a habit of constantly listening for the Sound. It is a matter of attention, and should be practiced all during the waking hours, during work and social activities, during everyday responsibilities and even — if possible — during the night.

When the attention is even subconsciously centered upon the Sound, or longing to hear the sound, it may come at any moment. Once the Sound occurs, you should not attempt to run after it, but keep the attention on the center of The Eye, and listen! Listen! Listen! Although it may not seem so, it is possible to subconsciously listen for the Sound and carry on one's obligations and duties. The attention should not be so completely diverted from duties that errors are made, but even while the whole attention is given to outward duties, still the mind can subconsciously "pray."

This is what the Master Jesus meant when he said to pray constantly.

(Words given in the Bible by Jesus regarding unceasing prayer, are: "Pray always," spoken on many occasions, as in Luke 21:36; Luke 18:1, etc. Perhaps the best known words quoted are those of Paul: "Pray without ceasing," (I Thes. 5:17) based on direct injunctions of Jesus.)

It is important to pray or turn the thoughts toward angels or spiritual teachers just before falling asleep. If there is no time for a long meditation, certainly the mind should turn toward the Nahd so that sleep is more beneficial. It is possible to attune to the Nahd during sleep, and this is by far the most peaceful rest possible.

Constant repetition — even subconsciously — of the Cosmic Mantra or the name of the Master, in addition to centering the attention in the Third Eye, is one of the secrets of attaining liberation, freedom from karma, and union with God. It is only through the human form that liberation is possible, and it is because of this that we attempt to evolve and perfect the human form, especially the brain, and the spiritual centers thereof.

It is quite possible that when one first begins to hear the Sound, it is frightening. The Sound does not always manifest gently or quietly, and may seem turbulent in its power. This does not indicate a need for cessation of the meditations, it means only that the physical frame is not yet attuned to withstand the force of the divine energy. And it is possible the Sound Current may come rushing into the head suddenly, when one least expects, causing various reactions. One should never be frightened at the intensity of the Sound. Keep the attention centered on the Sound itself. The angels and spiritual teachers are never nearer than when the mind is engulfed in such Current.

As meditation progresses, attunement to the Sound itself brings about a change in the frequency of the physical form, enabling it to align itself easily with higher vibrations. Eventually the divine energy permeates the entire body, raising the consciousness upward and inward.

It frequently happens that upon first hearing the Sound, a disciple will begin analyzing it. This is an error. Analyzing the Sound only defeats the purpose of the contact, which is to go inward and up with all of the mindforce. Analysis requires attention, thus diverting some of the mindforce from its inward journey. The mind should be given wholly and completely to the Nahd. When it does so, there need be no analysis because the Nahd itself will reveal all knowledge in time.

QUESTION: When one finally hears the Sound and is listening to go in deeper, should one continue to repeat the cosmic mantra aloud?

ANSWER: No. The mantra should be repeated mentally. Once the subtle Sound begins, concentrate all your attention upon it so that it may draw you further in and up. One of the first sounds heard may be that of a gong or a bell. Once this sound is experienced, hold the attention centered upon it. The Sound itself will have a pulling quality, helping the disciple to remain centered within.

QUESTION: Since the Holy Nahd is vibrating through all the atmosphere and the ethers, even permeating the body and the soul, why then cannot the disciple easily catch the Divine Sound?

ANSWER: The soul is immersed presently in the physical body, and since incarnating has attuned its hearing to the sounds of Earth, forgetting that there is the Sound of the Holy Nahd.

In order to hear the Nahd, the soul must become still, turning away from the sounds of the world and listening intently within. Only when the inner ear becomes attuned to the wavelength of the Nahd can the Sound be heard. Similar to tuning in a radio on the physical plane, the inner ear has a tuning device which must be aligned with the frequency of the Nahd. This can only be accomplished by turning deep within, and meditating on the Third Eye, which is the "radio mechanism" of the brain.

The disciple with the purified mind, the purified antakarana, hears the Sound easily. The best method to attain contact is to sit in solitude, place elbows on the upraised knees, place the thumbs in the ears and listen. This closes out all Earth sounds and aids in turning the entire attention toward the Sound.

QUESTION: How does one develop detachment yet remain true to family ties? How does one become "detached" from small children, for instance, who look to parents for security and love?

ANSWER: One of the principles of Lhama Yoga, the science of the Sound Current, is to cultivate detachment of the world and the things thereof. Such detachment is not meant, however, to disrupt family life. Devotion to God and the practice of meditation never implies disruption of family life. Rather, family relationships should be enhanced.

The aim is to live in the world, but not of the world; to develop a detached manner while still remaining devoted to family and daily duties.

The Holy Nahd — the Divine Melody — is the only thing to which the disciple should be attached. It is the link between oneself and God. But attachment to the Holy Nahd never implies a lack of responsibility for family life. One must learn how to love family without becoming attached as if members of the family belong to each other. No soul belongs to another.

QUESTION: How does karma bring us together with others? Is there a way to avoid becoming over involved with our relationships, focussing mostly on others instead of on ourselves and our own growth?

ANSWER: Karma is like the play of the wind upon the waters. Individuals drift together or apart — according to their past karmas, just as driftwood floats upon a river. Many pieces of the driftwood are brought together by the currents of the river, only later to be separated by a future current. This is the play of the karmas.

But those who truly love are never really separated, for when the fleeting drama of karma ends there is permanent reality always behind it, bringing together those for whom togetherness is meaningful.

But understanding the play of karma makes detachment and objectivity more easily attained. Holy Nahd has the power to detach us from people and things. When we are united with the Divine Melody, it becomes easy for us to rise above phenomena. We even learn to endure separations, knowing that the permanent Reality will bring us together again.

This is why the saints encourage disciples to meditate constantly, seeking interminably for connection to the Divine Current. Entering meditation and practicing Jap has a purifying effect, counteracting the play of karma. At this stage of our evolution, and while dwelling in the physical form, this is truly our only source of that which is changeless.

Grace and effort are inseparable. Without grace, effort is extremely difficult, if not impossible, and there can be no grace without effort. The disciple cannot depend upon grace alone. Such dependence makes one indolent, and s/he may cease to make personal effort. The disciple must use his/her

Holy Nahd

own personal efforts, and then pray that God sends grace. One without the other is impossible.

Chapter 8

Psychic Powers

QUESTION: I used to scorn the idea of looking to the end of the nose to develop clairvoyance and intuition. But lately I have tried gazing at the Third Eye and haven't as yet attained any great success with it.

I close my eyes and try to concentrate. And I find my mind wandering away more easily. But when I open my eyes and concentrate on the end of the nose, I've got a thing to concentrate on — a something! And I find that I'm able to hold my mind more centered.

ANSWER: For some people the end of the nose is the center; for others, the Third Eye, found in the middle of the eyebrows, is the center.

If you wish, paste something small between the eyebrows, at the point and time of concentration. That will help — not very heavy, just light. The object will exert some pressure. The pressure will draw your attention to that place.

In certain cases the nose-tip is better; in other cases, the center of the eyebrows is better. I like the tip of the nose very much. It crosses the eyes, creating an "image" upon which to focus the attention. It's a great stimulant to the Third Eye, to clairvoyance and clairsentience.

QUESTION: Do you cross your eyes if you choose to gaze at the end of the nose?

ANSWER: Yes. Your eyes will cross naturally when you gaze at the tip of the nose. But try crossing the eyes without thinking of the nose. You will see "diffused" images. Choose an object right in the middle of the images and concentrate on it. This is an extremely powerful method of developing clairvoyance. If you cannot hold the mind centered on the Third Eye, then choose this technique.

QUESTION: Please give some instructions on how to develop telepathy.

ANSWER: When two people are in telepathic communication, etheric manna flows along the aka cord between them, just as messages might travel over a telegraph wire. Clusters of microscopic thought forms are projected along the aka cord and perceived by the sender through the sixth sense, floating into the consciousness as subconscious impressions. Manna — electromagnetically charged force — once recognized and accepted, can be directed by the mind.

It uses aka cords, or threads, as perfect conductors far more successfully than electricity flowing over physical wire connections. These physical electric currents can only be projected certain distances before the "sending" weakens. But the manna-telepathic messages can be projected over currents of aka cord extending to infinite distances — to the cosmic dimensions of the incomparable human mind.

In telepathic practice, one becomes adept at projecting thought clusters along etheric threads connecting receiver and sender. We have previously taught of the aka cord radiating along the rays which flow from the eyes and the hands. It is easy enough to comprehend the existence of the manna and the aka cord extending between persons or objects — it is quite another to train the waking consciousness to become passive so that the sender can successfully project telepathic impressions.

Trainees are constantly projecting and receiving telepathically in their daily activities, learning how to maintain constant attunement with the waking conscious — not constantly attempting to send or receive, but to simply be aware of the occasional necessity to project a thought to a fellow seeker or to recognize the "receiving" sensation of a message reaching the consciousness.

When the sensation "vibrates," one must instinctively quiet the mind to receive an inflowing telepathic message. The sender frequently sketches the symbol on which s/he is meditating and projecting. The receiver should keep at hand a pen and paper to quickly sketch a symbol or note the words of the message. This seems to enable the waking conscious to more quickly develop telepathic powers.

First, a command must be made to the waking conscious of the sender that it is expected to perform, and then the subconscious mind of the receiver must become as passive as possible, so that it might receive what is being sent.

Once an etheric contact is established between sender and receiver, low voltage manna vital force is mentally projected along the aka thread. Thus, the invisible aka thread becomes electrically charged, and acts as a cosmic connection between the two brain centers. The sender is able to project along the low voltage aka wire and to observe the thoughts passing in the mind of the receiver. The images and thoughtforms flow again to the sender's center of consciousness, making him or her aware of the thought parade in the mind of the receiver. This same process can be followed whether or not the receiver is aware of being "read."

Along with these experiments, a trainee should sit in a completely darkened room and by placing the hands within several inches of an object, "read" its description. Or, completely blindfolded, walk through a room filled with furnishings and various objects, determining through sense perceptions how near you approach the objects, how far you were or are from them, the color of them, the shape, the meaning of them.

Telepathy for the Neophyte

When first seeking to unfold telepathically, the disciple may inadvertently experience some unpleasantness. Through inexperienced use of telepathic powers, one may occasionally tune in upon the weakness of a friend. Discerning a mistake on the part of another, one may react either as a judge or a tyrant, unless the disciple has also developed intuitively. First cultivating the intuitive quality develops a love aspect which shields one from reacting unfavorably to a friend's mistake.

One should not seek telepathic abilities as a means of gaining power over someone, but for sharing a mutual power with someone. Intuitive telepathy cannot be constructively applied unless there is a simultaneous unfolding of mercy, compassion, understanding and love. The first rule for unfolding telepathically is to acquire the attitude of sharing, not judging. The art of telepathy should tend toward intuitional spiritual purposes and not become sidetracked with petty personality interests.

The increasing ability of more and more people to communicate telepathically will be an incentive for humankind to adopt a guarded purity of life and thought, a persistent watchfulness over actions and ideas. Aware that a mental mirror may reflect one's thoughts gives pause for reflection.

Telepathy will call for a closer investigation of thought force, mind power and thought transference. Scientists investigating these mental activities will search for a transmitting channel and, it is hoped, discover the mental reflecting ether.

QUESTION: How does one go about achieving astral projection?

ANSWER: Astral travel differs somewhat from telepathy. When in mind reading and telepathy one is taught to project an elongated "finger" of the etheric form, creating an etheric aka cord. Whereas attempting astral flight, one must learn the discipline of projecting the entire soul-body, taking the center of consciousness along, leaving behind both the physical and the etheric double so that life might remain in the form. This presents more strict mental discipline, and involves considerable training.

All souls depart, to some degree, from their physical-etheric shells during sleep. These departures are actually astral journeys, most of which are seldom recognized as such, and seldom remembered. The secret of attaining the optimum astral experience is to project the astral form along with a portion of the subconscious, through which memory must flow to reach the waking conscious. In the majority of cases, the physical form and the waking consciousness must enter some degree of trance, so that all levels of awareness are projected, traveling to a destination either near or far away.

During the flight, the mind must be commanded to become extremely active, constantly projecting etheric threads to pick up scenes and thoughtforms witnessed and contacted, the better to remember the journey when the awareness returns to the traveler's physical form. That is the point of astral projection — to impress the waking conscious mind with the scenes witnessed and the thoughts observed during the flight.

The training and discipline for successful astral projection is difficult in that one must relax the physical self completely while, at the same time, strenuously projecting the soulforce from the body. Many are never able to accomplish it. In the Mystery Schools, the hierophant placed the neophytes in a state of hypnotic trance, giving the command that they would waken out of their bodies and be fully aware and capable of remembering. The neophyte would experience vague memories after repeated experiences. Further experiments sharpened the memory until the initiate-student was able to perform it alone.

Astral projection requires a gradual raising of the voltage of the vital force of the consciousness, frequently raising from low to mid-voltage, then increasing to high, if the astral self expects to journey any great distance into the higher astral and spiritual planes. Many fail to achieve it. Most find the voltage of the vital force is beyond their chemical endurance. If you find this to be true, you should cease attempting to train in conscious astral traveling — that is astral travel that will be consciously remembered.

QUESTION: How can we be sure of safe astral travel, or of perhaps attending training sessions Overthere to bring higher awareness into our consciousness?

ANSWER: The usual ascending consciousness is like the thistledown or the scattered substance of a dandelion, blown about by gentle winds during sleep. There is no direction, only vague drifting, scattered awareness. This is the ascension of the normal soul, and his/her dreams will be equally vague and scattered. This soul rarely ascends higher than the astral during sleep.

But the light seeker travels to a different drummer. Aware of journeys through higher realms, this soul will shoot like an arrow from a powerful bow to attain an ascended goal or plane.

The waking consciousness may have no awareness of a pre-arranged destination, but such a soul is under direct charge of its Oversoul, who will set up certain frequencies around the brain of the physical, which will direct the course of the ascending soul once the consciousness enters a sleep state.

Usually this soul, of its own choosing, will enter a realm of learning, sitting at the feet of a great one from the higher spheres. Or, s/he may speed to the site of one on Earth who is ill to administer healing. Or fly like a shooting star to some distant planet to gain knowledge of Earth's past, its future, or of spaceships and our ancient ancestors. Or seek awareness of yet other planes of existence. The light seeker's journeys may still seem vague upon waking, but they will have a greater impact upon the soul's evolution than that of the normal soul.

Beyond raising the voltage of the vital force, the most effective technique for these voyages of exploration is to focus awareness, just before sleep, upon higher realms, unseen teachers and goals to be gained. Or, simply open your soul through prayer to guidance from the Oversoul, who is wise to your needs physically, mentally and spiritually. And for protection, always invoke the affirmation, "I am surrounded by the Pure White Light of the Christ," or of the Divine Spirit.

QUESTION: Can you give one special exercise to develop psychic powers or ESP? — especially levitation?

ANSWER: In this levitation exercise, employ the chant for power: O-ang Shantee! In this instance, this chant is interpreted to mean "I am Master of myself!"

Stand erect, head up, heels together, hands at sides. Inhale a full yogic breath, raising the arms upward and outward to form the letter Y. As you raise the arms, rise on tiptoes, pull the navel in and up forcibly, and stretch as high as is comfortably possible. Lean against a support if necessary.

Now press the second and third fingers of each hand against the thumbs, straightening the index and small finger. Holding them erect, chant: O-ang Shantee-e-e-e! Vibrate the sound through the entire chest. Lower the arms as you begin to chant. As you lower the arms, imagine you are levitating the body, that your arms act as levers to lift the body through an imagined opening.

The arms should be tensed, but the rest of the body relaxed. As you gradually lower the arms, also lower the body. Keep the navel pulled in and up, concentrating power in the diaphragm and abdomen. This exercise and chant change the vibrations of your entire body, uniting you with a force of high voltage. Properly executed, you grow accustomed to perpetually feeling the presence of this indwelling power.

Repeat the exercise and chant seven times. After chanting, close the eyes and relax, but feel the power of the chant vibrating through you. Learn to chant silently even though you may not be able to perform the entire exercise, and imagine you are filling the whole of your body with this divine vibration. Continuing this exercise actually creates the feeling of mastership within you. It overcomes fear both of other people and of situations, as well as aiding the development of psychic abilities.

QUESTION: I have heard from mystical sources that when we are over a certain age that astral projection (such as astral travel etc.), cannot be learned. It has always puzzled me — why not? One should think that with advancing age and lesser interest in the material things, it should become easier. Can you shed some light on this for me?

ANSWER: You are right. As one "matures," one's thoughts automatically turn to the unseen world and all the mysteries and self-mastery connected with it.

Although there are techniques to master astral projection, very often it occurs without being "learned." It is a matter of soul development through one's lifetime — depending, of course, upon the lifestyle of that particular lifetime.

One's consciousness tends to seek for answers to the unknown as one matures, and included among that seeking is a subconscious upreaching toward a return to the home the soul left in the upper regions. That subconscious upreaching very often constitutes "a yearning" to project astrally. It behooves all of us as we enter the latter years of our incarnation to turn the consciousness full scope upon the unseen realm and the life to come. By so doing, we may automatically find ourselves remembering our "dreams" during which we automatically project astrally and bring many experiences back into full consciousness.

Good luck, light seeker. Regardless of Earth age, "maturity" of the soul and its level of achievement is soul progression, and it becomes easier as you grow spiritually, regardless of age.

QUESTION: What is the psyche? Is there a difference between the psyche and the soul?

ANSWER: Psychism is a doctrine of the soul. Since it manifests itself as an extension of the soul, the psyche and the soul are really one. The psyche possesses hidden powers that are potent and can be unfolded through certain techniques and mantric formulas. The seeker who possesses such psychic powers can transcend natural laws and perform "miracles" such as suspending the law of gravity, being seen in two places at the same time, assuming different sizes at will, mesmerizing, and other acts which some call "magic."

Helena Blavatsky declared that "magic is occult psychology, and the object of the art of magic is the perfection of man." Again she states that "magic is a divine science which leads to a participation in the attributes of divinity itself." The practitioner of white magic, being ruled by the Sun and using the five-pointed star, with the point uppermost, identifies with the true forces of evolution.

The psyche, or soul, means breath, life, soul, spirit, mind. It is the immortal part of us, the vehicle of spirit. The object of higher psychism is union with the divine, or at-one-ment with the High Self. It is the expansion of our consciousness from objective to spiritual. It is raising the vibrations of the physical body so that it will respond to the higher vibrations of the High Self. The motive of higher psychism is selfless service to humanity. This initiate consciously cooperates with the divine plan, and endeavors to further the will of the Planetary Logos.

The initiate uses yoga, meditation and concentration (for the waking up of one's pineal gland and the pituitary body) and thus develops spiritual perception — intuition, which will give insight into the processes of nature, and enable the initiate to use the powers of clairvoyance, clairaudience, telepathy, psychometry, healing, etc.

The initiate can ultimately control and manipulate deva substance with the cooperation of the great Builders. The initiate is able to contact them because of the purity of his or her life and the light of his or her vibration. Should one's body not be purified sufficiently and its atomic vibrations high enough to stand the strain, he or she could possibly overstimulate the chakric centers. The chakras are the mediators between the personality and the spirit. They are the portals of the psyche.

QUESTION: Why do most spiritual teachers advise one to go beyond psychic powers?

ANSWER: The development of psychic powers is a by-product of the ultimate aim of liberation. By all means, the seeker should treasure psychic powers if he or she will not make them the end of one's search. Through them, of course, one gains evidence of mind over matter, and proof that a disciplined mind can execute extra senses. But the ultimate aim is to free the soul from its entanglement with matter, releasing it to soar back to its source, the Father-Mother in heaven.

The only criticism of psychic powers is that too often the seeker becomes enamored of them, and forgets to go beyond them to the summit, which requires continued study, meditation and going within, the better to develop beyond the psychic powers.

QUESTION: Can you enlarge upon your previous concept of antigravity? Has your body ever levitated?

ANSWER: I'm not much of a scientist, but I do know that to neutralize the force of gravity so that the body levitates is related to the mind, mindforce and sound. The mind must first project a force powerful enough to neutralize the force of gravity in the Earth which holds us to the Earth. It is a mindforce science has not yet recognized, followed by a soundforce which changes the forcefield around the body.

There is also a universal force the scientists have not yet appreciated. My teachers call them particles — mind particles. And they refer to enzymes, and certain atoms. To levitate, one needs to cause the atoms to go opposite to the way they normally "travel." And that requires mindforce co-joined with the White Light. We must be able to generate a forcefield of White Light particles in order for human bodies to levitate.

Has my body ever levitated? Although I have practiced the levitation meditation earlier described, I have never been conscious of a physical levitation of my body. But when I sit in Padmasan yogic posture and pray or meditate, my mind sometimes rises to a different level of consciousness — and I feel my body rocking, rocking. Many rock while meditating — that's fairly common. But often I have felt the stirring of kundalini. It's like a grip and release, rocking back and forth. And I've felt the kundalini rise and strike my head through the right ear.

I'm sure my body did not levitate. I think one has to consciously make an effort, and my mind has been on other things. I try hard to hear the Holy Nahd. All I can say is, when we can generate more of the White Light into and around us — into our spinal columns — and when the kundalini force is ready for us to levitate, we can levitate — and perform other antigravity activities.

Psychic Powers

QUESTION: Is there a difference between psychic development (ESP) and spiritual Self-realization?

ANSWER: It is often difficult for the Western mind to differentiate psychic experience from spiritual experience. Both are classed generally under "extrasensory perception." However, psychic phenomena enjoys a wider field of investigation than does that of spiritual experience.

Psychic phenomena is usually related with Spiritualism, communication with those who have gone "beyond the veil," unfolding the psychic senses of clairvoyance, clairaudience, psychometry—whereas spiritual experience involves yoga, meditation, and the unfolding of spiritual faculties, such as the Third Eye.

While psychic experiences can be shared between a great many people as a group activity, spiritual experiences relate only to the individual's inner soul development. In any case, today in the West, considerable attention is given to both the psychic and spiritual aspects of our development.

QUESTION: What makes some people better healers than others? I want to develop my healing power, but need guidance.

ANSWER: You must first realize what happens in the body of a healer. As I make contact with my hands, either on your body directly, or while holding a prayer petition sent from a distance, I feel this magnetic or electric current going through my hands. I've been feeling this for a long time — this current going through my hands.

I've been praying my own version of the rosary which enhances this healing Force. If I want to be a great healer, I must attune my mind to a Higher Force. I must depend on a Force — call it my High Self, if you wish, which brings down into my consciousness a reverent — I want to say longing, but it's more than that — a magnificent obsession to heal. I want so badly to take the pain away. I automatically link up with a Divine Force coming through my mind that is of a reverent nature, so that when I make contact with your pain, something begins to happen in your body. The cells begin to absorb the enzymes and harmonize. The cells are like beacon lights, all together. The body begins to be filled with light, and more light. And you, in your asking and in your believing, begin to accept this magnetism that's pouring in, and my praying mind is charging your body with White Light — and this makes healing possible, depending upon whether or not the nature of your affliction is karmic, of course.

But, if you say, "I don't believe in an outside force. I don't need higher help," — when you start to think that, you'd better stop trying to heal, because you'll never really be a great healer. Until you link with a Higher Force or Divine Source, give it the credit and realize that without it you can do nothing — only when you can do that will you access the power to heal. Because one can heal only when the Force is coming through you, your hands fully charged with magnetism, the mind fully believing.

If patients come to you with full faith believing you have the power to "tune in" to the frequency of the White Light, and can accept it, then you can open their afflicted cells to become power plants — only then can you heal another. The patient may not be sure he or she is healed until the next time they visit their doctor who tells them they don't have the problem any more. The doctor may say, "What happened? What have you been doing?" You may say, "Nothing, I'm just feeling better."

Psychic Powers 173

You're reluctant to tell him or her you've been to a healer. But more and more people are telling their doctors, and more and more doctors are saying, "My gracious, that's wonderful. Whatever is happening, keep it up."

But if you really want to be a healer, pray, pray, pray for a Higher Force to overshadow you and help you help others.

Chapter 9

New Age and Evolution

QUESTION: John White, in an issue of *The Directory for the New World,* has written about a very provocative subject. It concerns the evolution of the future of humanity. He proposes the idea that the New Age brings forth a new species. When we talk about possible earmarks of the New Age and what we could expect, the answers indicate a pure love, a deeper caring about one another and about ourselves, a willingness to share. A willingness to network all over the planet, recognizing the trauma of change that is occurring all over the world. But still there is something that we as individuals and as a collective body might do. Are we really talking about the development of a new species of humankind?

ANSWER: I think it all relates to a cosmic transformation which will enable us to handle more energy, a new kind of lifeforce. We're not given this ability or this quality until we're able to handle it correctly. To have a new species, there must be a modification in human genes — in the DNA. This modification will take place all over the world, and the new species will be higher initiates born of a higher DNA.

Also, we must be aware that as those who long to remain in the Piscean Age vibration fall back, there are on the inner planes more highly evolved souls waiting to be born. As we see them being born on Earth in this Aquarian Age, we will become more aware of their wisdom, their love, because these will be innate qualities in these souls that have waited until this time to make their appearance again. Their births will probably presage the reappearance of the Christ and other avatars such as Moses, Buddha, Mohammed and Eastern Ascended Masters, with their energized spiritual forces.

But if there is to be a new species, there must be some kind of transformation. A transformation which would simply mean a higher plateau for the entire evolution of humankind. Since the new ones coming in are beyond light leaders of today, it means we will take a great leap forward. As the new ones with transformed DNA are born, and the new beings we will become gain critical mass on this Earth, we will certainly enter more dramatically into the New Age.

I have long been telling you that a new type of ether is entering our atmosphere — with extremely high frequencies. Well, these ethers are filled with a new type of lifeforce — we could even say a devic force. Devas are the elementals which indwell our plants, our trees, our mountains, even our waters. These new ethers are bringing in a higher type of devic elemental force, which is now entering our plant life.

As we humans consume these "new" plants, and breathe these ethers, a transformation will occur in our individual DNA files. We will be transformed into a new species. John White is right. These food plants will contain a force which will cause the human consciousness to "see" into a higher dimension. Gradually this transformation in consciousness will become the norm as human beings enter a higher level of the Aquarian Age.

I must tell you this story about Buddha after his enlightenment. One of the monks asked, "Are you God?" He said, "No."

"Are you a saint?" "No." And the monk said, "What are you?" He replied, "I'm awake." He was a new species. So was Jesus — whose father was "the Holy Ghost." Jesus was the first of a new species of the Aquarian Age. The human race will become "awake." Moses was "awake." Mohammed was "awake." So were the Eastern avatars, Krishna, Rama and others.

QUESTION: What distinguishes the form of human beings from all other forms?

ANSWER: Form is the vehicle through which the second aspect of the Logos manifests Itself within the Absolute One. The atoms which were built into forms by this Logos were the manifestation of the Holy Spirit, which is the third aspect of the Trinity. This manifestation was the first of our Solar System. We presently exist in the second manifestation, being that of the Son, the aspect of Wisdom-Love.

Form and life, matter and spirit, vehicle and consciousness, which are all synonymous terms, are one and inseparable in manifestation. They form the two indivisible aspects of the Absolute One.

Form can only exist because there is lifeforce ensouling it. Consciousness is the link between life and form. Form is the result of vibration. Vibration is the rhythmic motion of matter. By changing the rate of vibration, form is modified.

Form, having the lowest rate of vibration, is solid matter, and vibration having the highest rate, is Spirit. When this rate becomes infinite, the atoms of which the form is composed become omnipresent, form disappears and the many become One.

The purpose of form is to provide the vehicle through which

the soul and spirit may undergo self-imposed limitations, thereby acquiring experiences of the lowest and the highest rates of vibration. The processes by which this is accomplished are called involution, or descent into matter, and evolution or unfoldment, ascent from matter. Divine ideation passes from the abstract to the concrete as visible form. The subjective becomes objective, after which the process of evolution begins.

The within-form spirit is clothed in sheaths, and as it acquires the capacity to respond to the vibrations of the lowest world of form, it gradually abandons the sheaths one by one. It raises its level and becomes attuned to higher and higher vibrations, until all the sheaths are dropped—all form is abandoned and the imprisoned spirit finds its liberation.

Stated in terms of consciousness, the spirit passes from subjective to objective consciousness, and then to higher consciousness. In other words, it raises its consciousness to Self-consciousness, then to group-consciousness and finally to God-consciousness.

The form of a human being is different from all other forms first in its vertical posture, with its head toward the sun, receiving lifeforces or spiritual currents from above. Animals have a horizontal posture and receive their life energy from group souls. This energy revolves around the Earth. In comparison, plants have an inverted posture, but receive their life energies from both the Earth and the Sun.

Human forms have a highly developed brain and a nervous system which brings them into contact with a three-dimensional world, and the ability to participate in the fourth-dimensional, or spiritual world. Humans also have certain centers through which they may acquire spiritual perception. Finally, humans have a higher key of vibration than any of the forms of the lower kingdoms.

QUESTION: Humankind might be divided into the following groups: mundane beings; average beings; aspirants to knowledge; disciples; initiates; adepts.

Please define these terms, remembering that "all Paths lead to Me," says Krishna in the Gita, and that what the orthodox theologian calls religion is not the only way home. For instance, self-sacrificing service for humanity along the "way of science" is surely part of the way.

ANSWER: The six groups of humans in this question stand on six different steps of the ladder of evolution.

1. Mundane souls are those who live almost entirely in the physical plane consciousness. Their astral and mental bodies are in a low stage of development. They receive impressions from without, and know little about the existence of their inner Selves. They may have an idea of an external power or powers, which they may feel is divine, but this god or gods do not affect them in any other way except to cause them fear.

These souls seek to obtain all they can without any regard to consequence. If they unite with certain groups of other beings, it is only to form a united front to fight an enemy. If they protect their mates, it is in their own selfish interest. Thus they evolve their own individuality through their personality, and learn to serve in their own small and limited way. After these souls leave their physical vehicles they will continue their existence on the astral plane for a little while without perhaps much consciousness, and will reincarnate in a comparatively short time.

2. Average beings at the present time live mainly in the physical and astral worlds, and also in the mental world on a small scale. These souls are generally self-centered and live for the satisfaction of their desires. They have a personal God, about

whom they have learned in their churches or homes. They worship this God in order to gratify their desires and ambitions. These souls are, however, less self-focussed than the mundane. They love their families, their friends, their community and their country, serving them in order that they may be spared the punishment of everlasting hell, and perhaps enjoy the everlasting bliss of heaven.

Average souls today generally follow vocations in commercial or professional lines, through which they serve God unconsciously. They may be artists or scientists, and the service they render is in proportion to the sincerity, faithfulness and enthusiasm they put into their work. No matter what they are doing, if these souls do their very best to gain all the experience they can out of that work, they have followed the Path that leads to God.

After death, average souls will live longer in the astral plane, and perhaps in heaven for a short period, to assimilate the fruits of their labors, before returning to another physical life. Their consciousness will certainly be higher than that of the mundane, but they will not be Self-conscious on the astral and mental planes.

3. Aspirants to knowledge are those who have caught a glimpse of the spiritual world, an urge, a vision. These souls have come to understand that there are other states of consciousness which are more real than the one they are living in. They have learned of this great Reality. They have learned that to see this spiritual world, or be transferred to the higher planes, they must develop a new sense — intuition, wake up their energy centers and win "salvation" by effort.

In their daily lives aspirants to knowledge, or the neophytes, are those who are treading the path of probation. Most are not much different from the average being, except that they attempt to perform their duties more faithfully. These souls experience as much temptation as the average being — perhaps more. The only difference is that when the aspirants fall, they always rise again. These souls have learned to "know thyself," or their divinity, and all their endeavors are bent towards making contact with their Divine, or High Selves. They also have learned that the human family, nay, all life, is unified, and that any sense of separation with any other part of life is but an illusion. They know that the only way they can attain this unity or universal familyhood is through service. When the end of this short span of life comes, they meet death fearlessly, as these souls know there is a beyond where they will gather more knowledge and experience until they return to another incarnation, or a higher level on the spiral path of evolution.

4. Disciples are those who have offered themselves to a Master Teacher as pupils. This Master is first his or her Higher Self. Later on, it is those who have "mastered the law of cycles." The lives of disciples are quite different from that of aspirants in that they are cleaner, saner and truer. Their physical bodies are usually healthier, but not necessarily so. Their emotional lives exhibit healthy expressions of their emotions. They are Self-conscious in their emotional bodies, and can live and gather knowledge in these bodies.

Disciples, through meditation and prayer, have linked up their consciousness with their High Selves on the abstract level of the mental plane. Some of these soul's force centers are awakened. Their pineal glands are developed and have become the organ of spiritual perception, consciously employed. A disciple is Self-conscious on the mental plane, as well as on the physical and astral planes. When an incarnation finishes, he or she steps over consciously to the great beyond and continues to march toward Godhood.

5. Initiates are those who have expanded their consciousness to cosmic consciousness. They are given the "Key to Knowledge" by which they can open new vistas of wisdom and power to serve. Initiates can focus their attention in any direction and know anything they choose to know in order to serve perfectly. They feel all — therefore they can do all.

Initiates have cast off their personal selves and their sense of separation. They consciously realize that the Selves of all are one.

6. An adept is a high initiate. He or she is one who has passed the following five initiations:
- A. 1st — Cave of initiation (cave is the purified heart) - {He or she experiences a spiritual rebirth, kindling the fire of spiritual interest in the heart.
- B. 2nd — Baptism (Spirit indwelling) - {Kundalini awakened, passes from plane to plane without break of consciousness.
- C. 3rd — Transfiguration (initiation of glory) - {Unity achieved, no more births.
- D. 4th — Crucifixion (initiation of Calvary) - {Last fetter cast off.
- E. 5th — Resurrection (the triumph of the High Self) - {Omniscient Cosmic potency or planetary chain.

Please be sure to understand that these distinctions between mundane, average, aspirants, and so on have nothing to do with the amount of money one has, with IQ, with class, race or gender.

QUESTION: You have spoken in the Wisdom Teachings about the involution of the Monad through the plant, animal

New Age and Evolution

and human kingdoms — and then the evolution of the individualized human soul. Toward what purpose? To avoid reincarnating? You have called evolution a "ladder." Why?

ANSWER: The purpose of evolution, as far as the soul is concerned, is to produce the fully conscious, divine human being.

The "ladder of evolution" symbolizes the upward progression of the soul, the stages of spiritual progress. The poet, Joseph Gilbert Holland, also describes the "journey" as a ladder:

> "Heaven is not reached at a single bound,
> But we build the ladder by which we rise
> From the lowly Earth to the vaulted skies:
> And we mount to its summit round by round."

The law of evolution is the law of everlasting change. As far as it concerns the human race, it is the everlasting etherialization of matter, the unsheathing of the form, the unfolding of the soul, the spiritualization of the human. It is the continuous change of chaos into cosmos.

Anything that does not obey this law, or is inharmonious with it, destroys itself. Anything that is harmonious with it becomes part of the great stream of evolution, part of the everlasting progress.

We are told that 18 million years ago the Planetary Logos incarnated in a physical body, on the etheric plane, to assist, by His presence, the infant race of humankind, which had come to existence ages ago, making use of the animal form. Centers of souls were stimulated, and the first step for individualization was taken. (Again we are told that 60,000 million Monads were assigned to this evolution). It was then that the race of Self-conscious souls was born on this planet.

This newly born humankind began to develop "working consciousness" through its brain and nervous system. The soul thus developed a mind, and through its sense organs began to gather experiences through its sensations. The next step was to link the soul's sensations to physical objects, and thus it acquired perception. Then it used its memory, and by making mental pictures of the perceived objects, it formed ideas and concepts.

Then through comparing, or associating its different ideas, the soul began to reason and discover laws, such as the law of cause and effect, etc. Then it began to use the laws as instruments with which to consciously create, to command the forces of nature and make its own destiny.

While you, the soul, were progressing on the ladder of evolution, you discovered that you had an inner life as well as an outer life, and learned to turn within to find in yourself your Higher Self.

As you grew in your inner life, your emotional body began to assume a definite outline and grew into a more beautiful form. Your dream life changed. You acquired astral vision and experienced a glimpse of the higher life. This enabled you to understand your fellowbeings better, as you were not limited to outer senses alone, but could communicate with them astrally. You could also travel in your astral body in full consciousness and gather information from distant places. Astral manifestation occurred in the Atlantean period, and was an involuntary process. It temporarily disappeared during the development of the Manas, or levels of mind. During this period of the evolution of the lower mind, came the stage at which the majority of the human race is today.

Next your development will come in your causal body—the abstract mental body. Through concentration you will direct your thoughts and communicate with others by telepathy, without the limitations of the physical and astral bodies. You will create new forms, first mentally, then by the spoken word, as your creative energies are transferred to the throat centers. As you touch the abstract levels of the mental plane, you will make actual contact with your causal body and, for the first time, acquire the sense of immortality and become a conscious helper of the race on the mental plane.

We can say that the evolution of a soul is complete when it is able to function in unbroken consciousness, in five planes. When it has nothing more to learn from this scheme of evolution, it needs no more incarnations, except as it chooses to serve its fellowbeings. Space, time and matter disappear for you. You become a fully conscious being, a liberated soul.

This is the rough outline of the evolution of a soul to the highest development attainable by the soul in the three bodies. The evolution of the human race follows the same lines as that of the individual. At the present time only a few have reached their goal, but they have proved definitely that the law of evolution is working, that the goal is not out of reach and the time will come when all souls will attain liberation.

QUESTION: Why is all evolution in our solar system septenary in nature? Can you give examples of septenates?

ANSWER: Hippocrates said that the number seven, "... by its esoteric virtues tended to the accomplishment of all things, to be the dispenser of life and fountain of all its changes."

The basic principle of the universe is unity. The basic principle of creation or manifestation is duality. The aspects of life and of the Logos are in triplicity. Three will manifest itself in seven combinations, as follows: A–B–C; AB–AC–BC; ABC.

Seven is the number of perfection of form on all planes of manifestation. At this stage of evolution, there are seven main divisions with seven subdivisions.

From the point of view of number vibrations (numerology), seven stands for victory, perfection, synthesis, analysis; a gathering in, or assembling of life's lessons; the vehicle of life, nature's root number in the world of manifestation, introspection, consummation, attainment. People tuned to this number are said to be calm, refined and studious. They are idealists. But sometimes they are unreasonable, obstinate and autocratic.

Septenates

Seven types of Logoic energy, rays, power; seven types of substances or matter; seven states of matter; seven human and seven cosmic principles; seven creative hierarchies in active manifestation; seven streams of force in humans; seven cosmic planes and seven cycles; seven heavenly bodies — sacred planets; seven cycles in the age of a person, each period subdivided into seven years; seven centers in humans.

Seven days in a week; seven days in each phase of the moon; seven archangels; seven brothers, which are the seven planes of manifestation; seven Builders; seven chains in a scheme; seven cosmic initiates; seven cosmic paths; seven deva lords or raja lords; seven fires by friction; seven globes in a chain; seven heavenly beings; seven Kumaras; seven solar systems; seven planetary Logos; seven portals; seven root races and sub-races; seven sons of Fohat.

Seven stars of the Great Bear; seven vibrations ("Brothers of energy"); seven capital sins and virtues; seven eternities and seven periods; seven notes of the musical scale; seven colors; seven planes of cosmic consciousness; seven-stringed harp of Apollo; seven gods of Egypt; seven amshaspends of the Zoroastrians; seven as the holy and mystical number of Hebrews, as mentioned in the Bible.

Seven bullocks; seven rams; seven priests bearing seven trumpets; seven loaves; seven full baskets; seven stars in the right hand; seven golden candlesticks; seven angels; seven churches; seven spirits before the throne of God; seven angels of the Presence.

A perfect initiate is one in whom all the six principles have merged in the seventh.

QUESTION: What is the secret of celibacy and the conservation of sexual energy?

ANSWER: There is no secret to celibacy. I think everybody knows what celibacy means. I think the question could be, "What is the secret purpose of celibacy and the conservation of sexual energy?"

New Age seekers have been well taught concerning the shift in consciousness from the left brain to the right brain —bringing the right brain intuitional awareness into reality, the presence of the High Self into our lives through spiritual practices. This much sought after shift in consciousness takes place more easily when there is a conservation of sexual energies. Such conservation may stimulate the current of kundalini more quickly, which can then rise, strike the Third Eye and cause a shift in consciousness.

That's what happens during Astara's Fire Initiation, when, by the touch of the energy channelers on the Third Eye, a higher voltage of energy flows into it. Various sensations are experienced, depending on the openness of the soul standing before the one channeling the energy, and the connection between them. The higher voltage of energy causes the kundalini to stir and rise, creating a shift in consciousness. This sudden shift sometimes causes the person to fall backward. Many momentarily lose consciousness, see visions, hear music, travel in space, see the Clear Light, or experience a healing.

On an everyday level, we must consider that the conservation of sexual energies is for the purpose of stimulating kundalini, which is the feminine creative force. Kundalini is feminine. The Third Eye area is masculine. The "Father in Heaven" resides in the Oversoul. The Mother resides in kundalini.

When they unite in the Third Eye — when the feminine kundalini rises and the Father force descends — the pineal and the pituitary glands become active. They unite in a sexual union in the third ventricle of the brain, the Third Eye opens, the shift in consciousness takes place — stimulating the intuitive awareness, stimulating the Third Eye, stimulating the spirilla crystals in the pineal gland, uniting that crystal force to the fire of kundalini.

At this moment I'm seeing a fire, and in it a stone. And I see that the stone melts and becomes a fluid under the impact of the fire. My teacher means for me to interpret that for you. First, we have a conservation of sexual energy, which stimulates kundalini. The fire of kundalini rises up to strike the crystals — the stones — in the pineal gland, in the Third Eye. It's like a living fire which makes the crystals become fluid, creating a living White Light.

The White Light birth in the Third Eye can very rarely be accomplished without the conservation of sexual energy. So there are both the spiritual and the scientific reasons — the spiritual science — of conserving sex energy. I hope I've answered your question.

QUESTION: We are just beginning to learn about cloning. It seems that by saving some cells of the body a whole simulacrum of the person may be duplicated. Do you think the Ancients knew about cloning?

ANSWER: They not only knew about it, they set the stage for their greatest leaders to be cloned. That was what one phase of mummification was all about. When we have finally mastered the science of human cloning, it may be possible to take cells from the mummies of Egypt's greatest kings and pharaohs and clone their physical forms. But what we don't know is: will the spirit of that person come to ensoul that form? We should know that may require deep prayer. I believe it could happen — since that was the major purpose of mummification in the first place.

Wouldn't it be great to call Tut-Ankh-Amon to reinhabit his new form? Or Ramses? Or Seti? Or Zoser? Or Cheops? We surely could find out then that Cheops didn't build the Great Pyramid, and a great deal more about antiquity. But it is doubtful that the same soul would come back to inhabit the new form. And we may very well discover that human cloning is not advisable. There may be such an outcry against it, it will not happen.

QUESTION: You say that in the fullness of time we will not reproduce our offspring through the generative organs as we do now, but will instead become co-creators with God and reproduce through the spoken Word, as did God in the beginning. Can you explain?

ANSWER: In the early days of our evolutionary progression, when the spinal column first manifested in an upright position, development of the larynx and the brain became our most vital and principle activity as we sought to establish ourselves as human co-creators with God. A division of the generative powers was effected, a portion of them becoming resident in the generative organs at the base of the spine, a portion remaining in the brain. Thus the creative powers are still divided in humans today.

The larynx will gain increasing powers of creativity only as we, by our own will, are able to turn the generative kundalini forces in the root chakra, which hold us bound to the animal kingdom, upward. As the mind unfolds in the unending eternity ahead, just so will the larynx and brain be stimulated and developed until the upright larynx attains its full and powerful culmination, enabling us to create with the power of our own spoken word — even as do the gods.

Until we can propel the generative creative forces upward through the spinal cord we remain in a house divided — between the humans we are, and the gods we are to become.

QUESTION: In the Ancient Wisdom, isn't symbolism involved in the process of human evolution?

ANSWER: If we understood better the language of symbology, we would much more easily understand the language of evolution. The creation of humankind is thusly described in ancient Hindu literature:

"He (the Supreme) drew from His own essence the immortal breath which perisheth not in the being, and to this soul of the being, he gave the Ahancara (conscience of the ego) sovereign guide. Then he gave to that soul of the being (man) the intellect formed of the three qualities, and the five organs of the outward perception. The three qualities formed by the intellect are thought, perception and intuition. The five organs of the outer perception are the five senses."

Having decided to partake of mind substance and evolve into its own perfection, and, because of its choice, having been put out of their etheric existence to dwell in the world of matter, humans — finding themselves encompassed about with a coat of skin — imagined themselves to be apart from their God.

Witnessing the effects of the turbulent forces of the elements about them, they caused these forces to be given names pertaining to the animal kingdom. For they felt that the animals possessed powers far beyond those displayed by the human. It must be remembered, however, that they looked toward the animals of the heavenly zodiac when making this decision — not the animals of Earth.

Thus myth-making humans did not create the gods in their own image, but endowed them with the images of the kingdom of the zodiac — the animal kingdom. To more fully comprehend this phase of humanity's evolution, let's focus principally on ancient Egypt, for out of Egypt has come a vivid portrayal of humankind's primitive beginnings. As we understand Egypt and Egyptians, so shall we understand more of all evolution on the planet.

To ancient Egyptians, the gods and goddesses who arrived from other planets and walked among them represented the forces of nature. The beings of light strove to teach primitive human beings that the forces of nature were portrayed by zodiacal animals possessing superhuman powers, or demonstrating that which was beyond the human capabilities. But early humanity could not grasp so universal a concept.

To them, the powers and divinities of the gods and goddesses were first represented by birds, reptiles and animals of Earth, not some distant zodiac. For the infant human, whose footprints on the Earth plane first walked the valley of the Nile and Mesopotamia, recognized themselves to be too poor things after which to shape the superhuman powers of nature.

Indeed, early humans were so like animals themselves that had they, even with full intentions, imagined their God after their own likeness, God would still have been endowed with many animalistic qualities. So being, they found it better to choose animals with powers beyond their own, and to endow their gods and goddesses with the same type of superhuman powers. It was much later that the gods of mythology came to be clothed in human likeness.

Our ancient ancestors were too awed by the powers of the elements to conceive of them being their likeness in any way. The mind of the early human gave birth to a sign language, depicted in hieroglyphics. Misinterpretation and an ignorance of the meaning of these hieroglyphics has led to many false beliefs and many misconceptions concerning the originators and writers of the ancient sign language.

Out of ignorance of their hieroglyphic symbols, which recorded thoughts, concepts, stories, transactions, and histories in picture form, the ancient Egyptians were accused of worshipping objects and animals. They have been called moon worshippers, sun worshippers, serpent worshippers, crocodile worshippers, bull worshippers, tree worshippers and phallic worshippers. And to a great extent, they were.

The crash of the thunderbolt through the heavens, the flash of lightning that struck terror, the force that caused the fire to be hot and destructive, the power in roaring flood waters and the scream of the wind in a hurricane were all superhuman powers, and were represented as such in hieroglyphic writing. So also were the animals and birds, which the ancients used to depict the mysterious elemental powers — the powers manifesting in air, fire, water, earth, thunder and lightning.

Later, when the human form began to be used to depict gods, and mythology began to develop, masks were placed upon the forms to depict superhuman powers — but not the powers of Earth animals, but, rather, again, the animals of the zodiacal heavens. But the animals and symbols so chosen were not objects to be worshipped; they were simply a means of expressing the feeling concerning the elements.

These ancients described the processes of life in the language of animals. "I have become a lizard," declared the young woman at the time of puberty — meaning she had left her childhood and had entered her womanhood — she had become capable of childbearing. The lizard symbolized such a transformation.

"I am turned into a frog," said the woman whose monthly period was upon her. The symbol of the frog was used, not because it was worshipped, but because she had undergone, for a few days, a certain type of transformation. The Native Americans felt that the frog symbolized cleansing, for it is the frog who sings the song which calls the rain to come and cleanse Mother Earth.

Other modes of progress were described when the person became a beetle, a bull, a bear or even the lotus. The most ancient of all mantras, "Om Mani Padme Hum," translates "I am the jewel in the lotus," which certainly does not imply that the personality has become either a flower or a jewel — but describes an inner process of spiritual attainment and transformation.

Modern humans speak of a man in the moon. The Indians of Northwestern America declare there to be a frog in the moon — which implies to them that the moon is constantly undergoing transformation, as is woman when she temporarily becomes "the frog."

Modern writers of mythology declare the scarab to be an object of worship in ancient Egypt — that it was a symbol of divinity. But even a minute contemplation will obviously reveal that the beetle only symbolized the divinity that was worshipped. Most certainly the beetle itself — the scarab — was not the object worshipped. Here again, the scarab symbolized a form of transformation accomplished by Ptah — the divinity that was worshipped.

QUESTION: Along what lines is the human race evolving toward higher consciousness?

ANSWER: In this life of eternal search there are three main lines of thought along which we are trying to expand our consciousness. These are scientific, religious and philosophical-mystical. Since the object of all three is to find Truth, they should never be antagonistic to each other. Ignorance and intolerance sometimes create antagonism. But when it is understood that science, religion and philosophy are all paths leading to the same purpose — each from different angles — and since no one method has a monopoly on the Truth, all antagonisms should cease. Tolerant people agree to differ, but they never become antagonistic.

Let's now examine these three lines of thought and their relation to one another.

Science is classified knowledge, and concerns itself entirely with the form, the material or objective side of manifestation. Its methods are observation of facts, gathering of knowledge through the five senses, analysis of such knowledge, classification, discovery of laws governing the phenomena by induction, and verification by experiments.

As positivistic science is not concerned with facts which cannot be observed by the physical senses and by physical experimentation, it is extremely limited. Experiments must be made by instruments made of matter, and all matter has its limitations. Consequently, scientific progress is very slow.

There was a time not long ago when science considered the atom to be indivisible, since no instruments had been found for its division. With the discovery of radioactive substances and the advancement of the science of electricity, the entire atomic theory was revolutionized, and an immense field was opened before the physicist to further investigate the laws of matter and energy. The discovery of cosmic rays opened up still a new field of investigation into the etheric world. Transmutation of elements is now seen under a new light, and images are received from vast distances.

Religion is the communion of humanity with its God. It is concerned with the spiritual side of manifestation, with that which is subjective. Spirit being intangible cannot come under observation and laboratory experimentation. It is known only as we become aware of it intuitively. Since the consciousness of different souls vibrate on different levels — no two consciousnesses ever being alike — the intuitive knowledge of different souls also differs somewhat.

Hence, religion and science are like the opposite poles of a magnet and seemingly contradictory to each other. Science gathers knowledge from the material universe. Religion seeks wisdom concerning the spiritual world. Science analyzes fact and investigates natural laws — religion synthesizes the spiritual experiences of individuals and thus expands their consciousness. Science deals entirely with matter, religion with spirit —

and this very act of separating matter from energy, or spirit, is a great barrier to the advancement of religion.

Philosophy, which concerns itself with both the intellectual and mystical side of manifestation, links the above two seemingly polarized viewpoints together. It is the relation between, and harmonizing element of the two. Philosophy seeks to prove that the within and the without, the spirit and the form, energy and matter are one, and only different phases of the same power, like the positive and negative phases of electricity; that the scientific and religious views taken separately cannot be the complete expression of Truth, that these views are complementary to each other.

Orthodox science and orthodox religion have actually limited their scope by refusing to see phenomena which occur daily. One, because these manifestations do not come under laboratory tests, and the other because they are confined by the Bible or the dogma they believe in. Philosophy's purpose is to erase these scientific and religious prejudices.

It is the philosopher-mystic who broadens the field of the scientist, leading him or her into the realm of the unseen, and shows the religious that matter is not something to be despised. The philosopher seeks to convince the religious that matter is as holy as spirit. It is crystallized spirit, and it is not blind faith alone that leads us into the discovery of the unseen. It is the function of philosophy to lift up the veil of ignorance and prejudice and to bring us to an understanding of the One and All.

QUESTION: Something I have wondered about is transplanted organs. What happens to seed atoms when a transplant takes place?

ANSWER: The seed atoms are etheric. They remain with you at all times — no matter what happens to your physical body. If you have a heart transplant, your heat seed atom remains with you. The emotional seed atom is in the apex of the liver, and it always stays with you, as does the mental seed atom, in the pineal gland. They all remain with you when you die and come with you if you incarnate again. These three seed atoms, along with the soul, bring the karma enmeshed in them according to the life you're living now. So do not worry. You will still have your seed atoms, no matter what organ is transplanted.

QUESTION: My son had an accident when he was 13 years old, in which he lost his spleen. He is now a healthy 29. Since the chakric force is influenced by the glandular operation in the individual (and vice versa), what happens to the prana when a person has had their spleen removed? You write that "When a gland and its corresponding chakra become disconnected, the flow of etheric energy into the dense physical form is obstructed or cut off entirely." Is my son's navel chakra dead, or non-functioning in this case? Can it be stimulated or revived in any way without a spleen?

ANSWER: The chakras are force centers of the etheric body, or etheric double, which is an exact duplicate of the physical form, but composed of four higher physical substances we call ethers. The chakras, or force centers, of the etheric body superimpose and interpenetrate the glands of the dense physical form. These force centers indraw the solar, pranic and lifeforces of the atmosphere and pour them into the physical form.

The chakra associated with the spleen is located two inches below the navel, and is sometimes called the navel chakra. These energy tubes, or "sockets," are connected directly to the ganglia on the spinal cord — in other words, a mass of nerve cells serving as a center from which impulses are transmitted, a center to which energy interpenetrates to the glands of the physical body. The removal of your son's spleen would not affect the splenic-navel chakra because the etheric chakra extends beyond the spleen into a center directly beneath the navel. I pray this eases your mind, and brings about a clearer understanding.

QUESTION: As we enter the Aquarian Age, does it mean we must be able to transcend time and density in order to function as a New Age person?

ANSWER: So long as this planet manifests in the field of matter and we assume these forms of matter, we are subject to time and space and density. Our initiations, at the present, are only in consciousness. We can transcend time in consciousness. We can transcend space in consciousness. But we must do so in dense physical bodies. The New Age is the space age of spaceships. In that sense we will transcend time.

As Earth itself enters its initiation — the new ethers of Aquarius — there will gradually come a space and a time when the matter of this Earth will begin etherealizing. Our human forms will begin etherealizing. We will occasionally dwell then on the level of the etheric body, and on the level of the etheric plane. Then we will manifest gradually back and forth for a time between time and space, learning how to transcend both. And there will come a time when both the planet, and the human lifewave of this planet, move totally into the etheric plane. Only then will we thoroughly be able to transcend what we know as time and space as it relates to the world of matter.

The Aquarian ethers now entering our atmosphere are already affecting our minds — as they penetrate our food and as they affect us through breathing. Our "old ones will see visions and our young ones will dream dreams" — as the Bible says we will do. We'll begin to respond to visions and spiritual forces — especially the light seekers. The visions may seem similar to the psychedelic experiences some had during the 60's, except they will come about as a natural happening, instead of through drugs — because our soil and the plants we eat will be saturated with these new ethers. And our breathing will respond to the ether's effect on our cells, our atomic structures and our bloodstreams.

QUESTION: What is the ultimate goal of the New Age seeker of light?

ANSWER: This can best be answered by a channeling I received when a certain seeker of light asked this question of her teacher many years ago. The teacher wrote:

"When you first became a seeker of light, you entered a new epoch in your spiritual evolution. As a member of the outer Lodge — 'The order of Melchizedek' — you acquired knowledge that you deemed profound and marvelous, through your studies and seeking. As you advanced, you acquired knowledge that was even more amazing in its scope and usefulness. You began to taste the waters of the hidden fountain; and, after a certain time in your studies of Ancient Wisdom, you wished to enter more definitely into cooperation with the Great Purpose as it is being unfolded in the Aquarian Age. You were invited into the inner order of Melchizedek. No greater honor than this last could come to you in a mystical way, unless it is to become an immediate member of the Melchizedek Lodge of the World in full consciousness. Of course, as a light seeker, you were a *chela* in that Lodge already. Membership in the Great White Light Lodge of the World in full consciousness implies an actual contact with the Masters of Wisdom in their permanent retreat.

"But to return to our mention made above to the 'waters of the hidden fountain.' This Arcana, together with the secret work of the New Age Mystery Schools, will eventually lead all seekers through portal after portal of initiation and onward up the sweeping stairs of life to the very Throne of God. The knowledge now pouring through from the divine hierarchy is the Divine Wisdom known throughout the universe.

"In the beginning of your seeking, you found yourself at variance with that which was imparted to you in the outer Lodge. But you were in the outer court with many to whom the pellucid fountain springs could not be revealed completely. But once one is found worthy, Truth is revealed in all her beauty.

"Cherish, then, these treasures, and value them well; for in them lies the essence of happiness together with that peace which passeth understanding."

QUESTION: Do angels ever incarnate, or is their evolution separate from ours?

ANSWER: There are some angels who did incarnate and who evolved to a particular high state. They then could elect to join the Angelic Force and help those still on Earth, and souls after they make their transition. There is another angelic race that never has and never will be incarnated in Earth bodies. They

New Age and Evolution 201

are on a different evolutionary wave than ours. There are some souls who have gone through the evolutionary Earth progression and have become a part of an angelic force. But usually those beings we call angels — have never been, and never will incarnate on Earth. They are protective, guardian angels.

Chapter 10

Tomorrow-ward

QUESTION: How do present world crises effect our individual soul progression?

ANSWER: So much of world thought today seems focused on the conquest and exploration of outer space, projecting into the great yonder our missiles, our satellites, our moon ships, our sky spies. We seem preoccupied with conquering outer space and too often we seem to be neglecting our inner space. So busy is science developing the potential of the material atom, the masses find little time to search the mysteries of the "human atom" — the soul itself.

We barely stop to think of the metaphysical atmosphere lying closer to the Earth, an atmosphere, an aura made dark from humanity burning its carnal refuse. It is the result of humanity's evil, our hatreds, our greed, our petty ambitions.

Those entering a wider vision and witnessing the appalling truth of Earth's affliction stand dismayed, wondering how we can achieve an escape, an exit through the clouds and into the upper light. It remains for the individual seeker to build his or her own mental missile and send it soaring into the higher regions, there entering its orbit. Your own personal missile, your own individual spaceship, your own mental satellite can keep you in touch then, telepathically or electronically, with the higher planes of life, can help you transcend the atmosphere about us and keep contact with thoughts of love and light.

The New Age seeker views science and religion and becomes incredulous at the vision. Science still stands shaken by its own discoveries. Scientists have exploded the atom and seen that the world of matter is built completely upon illusion, just as the great sages have always said. They see before them a laboratory of ethers and strange, curious elements. But they fear to let go of matter because it represents to them their whole world, and their level of understanding cannot grasp the science of the ethers.

Turning hopefully toward religion, the seeker finds that many churches have made of God only a Great Man endowed with human attributes and qualities, instead of inspiring their followers to seek for the God within themselves.

Some centers of worship, under the guidance of their spiritual leaders, enter a frenzied round of social escapes — suppers, bazaars, bingo parties, anything except facing the reality that they are not revealing to their people the God which they should seek.

Leading a seeker in a ceremony of meditation and teaching the infinite powers of one's own mind are not socially popular in churches today. So for many, religion has become largely a source of social communion.

It remains, then, for the individual to find his/her own path to God and into the light, despite the distraction of Earth's problems. Such a seeker recognizes the presence of the battle of Armageddon, the battle of the light against the dark, the battle of the mind which has generated some degrees of light, as opposed to the forces of darkness pressing upon us. The battle cannot be won with weapons or on a battlefield, but only as each seeker so projects his or her personal light that it may disperse some share of the darkness. Thus each seeker shares in bringing to birth a New Age religion which, unafraid to face the power of the atom and its implications, will help to reeducate the world to the power of the human atom and its dynamic potential.

QUESTION: In October, 1977, a new planetoid, Charon, was discovered at Palomar Observatory. What is the significance of this new energy upon humanity? Is another planet about to make its presence known?

ANSWER: Charon is really Pluto's moon, so named from Greek mythology after the boatman who operated the ferry across the river Styx to Pluto's realm in the underworld. However, there will be a new planet and it will affect you greatly. This new planet or asteroid certainly will change life on Earth by somehow creating a dimensional shift.

It's presently well beyond Pluto — the furthest out of the planets in our solar system. Perhaps we are not yet able to see it with the equipment we have at present. I do know we will one day, at some point before it has any impact upon our lives, develop the technology to view this new heavenly body. We'll have to wait until we build the telescope whereby we can view it. This new planet will greatly accelerate the ethers and energies of our own planet as Earth passes into the Aquarian Age, affecting our human lifewave so drastically that all incoming souls will be influenced. A "new" type of being will be coming into birth, and the old type will begin to fade away. Only the advanced souls of a new race will be able to inbreathe these new Aquarian ethers — both Earth and humanity will enter a prophesied period of peace and blessedness.

In no way is there a cataclysmic event connected to this new planet. It is not to be feared, but to be embraced for its influence on the human lifewave.

QUESTION: I'd like to know more about the mind being a sixth sense?

ANSWER: Senses are organs by which we become aware of our surroundings and through which we become aware we are sentient beings. They are the media by which souls, using their physical nervous systems, come into contact with their environment. Our senses are the result of our desires, our needs, of a spiritual urge to know, to grow, to unfold, to come into contact with that most mysterious and most wonderful thing called life, with its pains and sorrows that purify, teach and strengthen — and its pleasures that harmonize all our vehicles and permit the Self to express Itself, to grow and become illuminated.

The common senses, in their order of spiritual development and relationship to ego, are: hearing, touch, sight, taste and smell.

Mind is considered to be the sixth sense. It is the synthesizing faculty, or sense. Like the sense of sight, it gives us an idea of the proportion of things. It enables us to compare things, clarify them and discover the relation between the Self and not-self.

QUESTION: Can you tell us more about the sixth sense? How does it help us to find our identity with the One Self?

ANSWER: The mind, as the sixth sense, includes the aspect of intuition, a sense beyond that of our everydayness, and a link to the High Self. It embraces the soul-senses of clairvoyance, clairaudience and clairsentience, which are all attributes of the High Self. We become sixth-sense creatures as we develop our oneness with our Oversoul, as we gain more and more of our Self-illumination.

It is through the mind that the individual, or the ego, first perfects the personality. We see the Self in many forms, and after the forms are perfected, after the veils that hide the Truth are removed, our identity with the One Self is revealed. We then can consciously reject the not-self as an illusion and strive to unify ourselves with the One — the Absolute.

It is through the evolution of the senses that the individual rises out of the world of illusion into the pure realms of "Truth." The mind is an instrument of the soul.

QUESTION: Did your teachers ever instruct you in tonal qualities to attain greater spiritual development?

ANSWER: There is a basic law of attraction — like attracts like; like creates like; like responds to like. There are three basic tones of the human voice. The tones can be caused to vibrate, depending upon where one deliberately focuses the vibration in the body.

The Mental Tone

This tone suggests mental conflicts — and should be focused in the center of the head and upper chest.

It should be used for only three purposes:
1. to attract attention;
2. to present information;

3. for explanations which awaken keener perception.

This tone should be judiciously used by teachers for instructional purposes and not for self-aggrandizement.

The Feeling Tone

You can always convey your feelings by the tone employed. The feeling or emotional tone should be used to convey to the listener a true picture of your compassion, your kindness, your courtesy, your desire to serve. It should always be used when you attempt to persuade someone to follow your suggestion.

Employ the deep emotional tone from the center of the solar plexus near the heart. Use this tone in working with others. Use it in any interview in which you seek employment. As you use it, concentrate upon the vibrations of the chest. Feel the tone vibrate through the chest. Place your hands approximately at the level of the heart in the middle of the chest. Then speak aloud, lowering your voice, so that you feel the vibration of your tone underneath your hands.

Speak quietly, as if you were addressing someone very dear to you. When you use this tone, it is less likely that anyone will conflict with you, or be annoyed with you. Nor can you react with annoyance when using this love tone flowing from the heart region.

The Power Tone

This tone should always be projected from the abdomen and the big muscles at the waist. The use of these muscles adds power to any phrase or sentence or expression. Center your attention there, and project the vibration from the abdominal region. Use this tone when making demands or giving commands.

Coming from the abdominal region, your tone will pack a "punch." With every phrase you project, imagine that you are delivering a positive, but kind, impact just under the ear, or on the chest, or between the eyes.

At the same time you project your tone, keep it low pitched. Employ this tone when you wish to secure justice. You cannot attain your desires by shouting or using many words. Successful lawyers employ this tone.

Developing the Three Tones

1. The Mental Tone

Inhale a short breath in the top of the chest. Concentrate the tone in the middle of the head, and chant: O-ang. Keep the tone high pitched in your head. Use this high pitched mental tone only when you wish to gain attention. Then, after you have gained attention, drop the pitch of your voice, lowering to your emotional tone.

2. The Emotional Tone

Inhale and fill the upper chest, and concentrate your attention on the heart region. Concentrate on making your tone express your kindness and love. To do so, chant the syllable O-ang. Keep the tone low pitched. Practice until you feel the vibration throughout the heart region.

3. The Power Tone

Inhale deeply, filling the chest with air. Place a hand over your navel, and quietly state your intention. Chant O-ang. Keep the tone low pitched again. Continue practicing until you can feel the vibration of the chant over the abdominal area. Practice until you are able to employ these three tones for any purpose you desire.

Never speak habitually in a high pitched mental tone. Many people do. These are the people who suffer failures and afflictions caused by tension in the neck muscles. They usually have problems dealing with others. By changing the tone and lowering the pitch of the voice, the vibration is automatically lowered. The throat muscles relax, and tension disappears.

Practicing this exercise results in greater success in dealing with others and in developing your own inner spiritual qualities.

QUESTION: I have just finished studying your teachings that the brain is like a computer — an instrument through which the mind pours information, like a radio. Can you enlarge upon this? Now that the whole world is turning to computers the teachings seem to be extremely important, even to scientists.

ANSWER: My teachers have, indeed, channeled a great deal about this important understanding. They teach that the brain contains various centers — neurons — of cells related to various human activities and talents — such as the speech center, the hearing center, the sight center, even the bliss center. And there are special talent centers developed through training which pianists, engineers, writers, dancers and those with various skills display. The training creates special brain centers for each skill.

The teachings speak of the seven minuscule crystal magnets found in the pineal gland which act much as computer chips. Each crystal is called a spirilla, and each developed during long periods of evolution.

The masters have revealed to me that as each center of the brain develops, it acts much like a "programmed" computer chip. And they taught that in the future, by having a special crystal chip inserted in the brain, one could obtain the equivalent of a college degree — a degree in engineering, or training as a physician, etc. — almost overnight.

Lest anyone think this omits God and the soul, be aware that the use of these crystal chips appear to be part of God's great plan for us. These crystal magnetic chips will bring about astonishing advancements in the human race, and are part of God's evolutionary path for us. Perhaps this is why the Divine Spirit brought about the computer revolution. Actually, their teaching about the three permanent seed atoms could be compared to divine computer chips, programmed by you during all the lives you've lived as a reincarnating soul — and by God.

Scientists already know there are miniature magnets in the brain. We'll soon discover many of them to be crystals. Some of these chips could be like crystal receiving sets, allowing us to download information. Others would enable our physical manifestations to remain young indefinitely, transforming and changing the need to incarnate. There will also be crystal chips that will enable us to receive communications from the other planes of existence — and perhaps direct contact with the godbeings now assisting our evolution.

QUESTION: Do you expect a World War within the next 20 years?

ANSWER: No. I think enough of us will say the prayers requested by the Blessed Virgin that the White Light we generate will balance out the forces that would cause the war. I think we shall see continuing change in Russia. I think the Mother is going to have a major impact there. I think Medjugorje and the Mother's messages are going to change the world. I believe we will not have a third World War. But we do have other major problems. The Mother warns of a world catastrophe unless the human race turns more Godward.

We need to be aware of the greenhouse effect, the ozone layer, world pollution, overpopulation, our contaminated oceans, melting glaciers — things that have nothing to do with a world war. What we have done to ourselves and the Earth is as destructive as war. At least it's as bad — except maybe, maybe, maybe we can stop it and reverse it.

How do we rebuild to ozone layer? It takes more than trees. Only God knows how. Only God's mercy will strengthen the ozone layer again and protect us from the ultraviolet rays of the sun. I have great faith that light seekers are praying. The divine forces of light are depending on us to say the prayers to help change our direction and heal our home rather than harming Mother Earth and one another. We must do our part. It needn't be the rosary, but say some type of daily prayers for global healing peace. Do send out a force which helps raise the vibration of the planet and all of life into more and more light.

That's the only way we shall heal the world and turn away from simply repeating negative patterns from humanity's history. Ending pollution and healing our planet, respecting Mother Earth for all the spiritual energy she offers us, is one of the most important goals we can all work toward.

QUESTION: A Russian named Nikola Tesla supposedly came up with some pretty astonishing inventions, some of which are said to harness cosmic forces. When he died, did Russian agents abscond with all his papers, drafts and ideas, or did our government in Washington keep some on file?

ANSWER: No one has a certainty of what happened to them. Rumor has it that Russian agents took most of them for the purpose of putting his ideas to practical use. Those kept by the United States were filed away for the purpose of *not* putting them to practical use. Tesla died in 1943.

It is well known that the FBI did take some of his papers. Rumor again says that a microfilm file of all his papers is hidden in the National Archives. But no lay person can say for sure.

In Arnold Matthew's book, "The Wall of Light," he published a diagram of Tesla's Telescope. The Telescope was a device with which Tesla planned to communicate with people from other planets. It must have contained a geiger counter-like device, because it detected cosmic ray signals. Scientists say that Earth is constantly bombarded by these rays, evidenced by transducers which receive signals.

To this day, our government has never unveiled Tesla's knowledge of harnessing cosmic energy to heat and light our homes. They refuse to reveal such knowledge because they believe such inventions would wreck our economy. With such devices we would receive cosmic energy at no cost and not have to pay for lighting and heating our homes and offices. That would never do!

Free energy would simply change the world. At any rate, whether we or the Russians have his papers, Tesla's secrets are still being kept under wraps.

I have a distinct intuitive impression there will soon be destructive forces at work to demolish the sources of oil production in the Middle East, forcing this nation toward alternative energy — automobiles functioning with a fuel other than gasoline, and airplanes, too. By the year 2,000 we may see some of Tesla's plans begin to surface.

QUESTION: Do you believe it is necessary for all of humanity to purify the Earth, or must the purification of each one of us be an automatic or individual thing because of the change of awareness?

ANSWER: I think it begins with individual awareness and then becomes a group effort. Awareness is a personal thing. I think we absolutely must change personally — no one is going to make us change our diet, for instance — that's a personal thing. I can speak here to you about the importance of nutrition, but that doesn't mean you will believe it or will go home and do it. It's an individual thing. No one is going to force another to become a New Age light seeker.

We do have the down pouring white lighted ethers coming in to be of help to us. The planet itself will help in the Aquarian Age purification. But we must do our part to purify ourselves and our planet. If we do not, we are hastening our own destruction.

Purification means working for peace and understanding between people, classes, races, cultures and countries. It means turning away from old violent ways of resolving conflict, and searching for peaceful ways which promote justice and tolerance. It means praying for these things and acting on them in our own lives as we strive to enhance our individual spiritual growth.

The new type of Aquarian ethers into which the planet is now moving means many souls may be unable to continue incarnating on this planet. So each individual must seek self-purification if that soul wishes to enter the Age of Aquarius along with the planet.

At the same time, as we seek self-purification, we become more aware of the necessity to cleanse, heal and protect our planet. Each of us must work individually and collectively to do so.

QUESTION: Are we now experiencing the chastisement Mother Mary prophesied long ago, and even recently?

ANSWER: Our Lady of Light has pleaded for years for more prayers to prevent world chastisement. She led the struggle to collapse the threat of communism, so the fear of that is no longer there. Trust her to help also in bringing about the restoration of world enlightenment. She has said at Medjugorge, "I have a Great Plan!" She also said, "Pray for my intentions with the love you have for me, so that every plan of God about each one of you may be fulfilled." Such magnificent words. Prayers will help her bring her "intentions" to fruition.

She certainly is here among us. She is appearing at many places. She is preparing for the return of the Divine Spirit to visit our Mother Earth again. There may be some phases of "destruction," such as earthquakes, volcanos, droughts, etc. There are now thousands of starving babies and children because of the population explosion. There is far too much poverty. I'm sure she didn't plan that. These things may be a part of the chastisement.

But she continuously warns concerning mass chastisement if humankind does not turn Godward. Our own dear country — and every other — lanquishes under a spiritual ambiguity and a great vulnerability to the baser natures of humankind. It's hard to know whether this is a phase of the chastisement she spoke of.

I can't answer that for you. You'll have to make your own decision. I can only say I pray daily for Our Lady's "intentions," whatever they are. She knows — and I trust her and her Great Plan. I urge you, however, to avoid taking up your time and energy living in fear of disaster. Instead, be a light bearer yourself. Focus on the divinity within you and every living being. Send light to all the Earth and pray. Use your time and energy in this way, moving forward in trust and hope. This will be doing the Mother's bidding, working with the divine energies within you for your own soul evolution and the evolution of the entire planet.

QUESTION: In your earlier writing you said a special Hall of Records, once housed in Tibet in subterranean caverns, would be moved to the Andes. Have they been moved? Where is the temple, and where are the records now?

ANSWER: I remember when I wrote much about Kuthumi, much about Shigatshi in Tibet, where he once dwelt. He has now left the physical plane. In the Valley of Shigatshi there was, and is, a tremendous underground cavern where books and ancient manuscripts were, and are stored. There are still vast Records left underground in Tibet. They will stay there because of the cavern's inaccessibility. And they will remain inaccessible until divine forces want them found.

There is another Hall of Records at Lhasa, with an underground cavern. The Dalai Lama and the lamas of Lhasa know about it, but rarely enter it physically, preferring to travel there astrally, in their etheric bodies. The lamas can sit in trance, leave their bodies, travel to the chosen cavern and access the Records.

And I remember saying there would come a time when the Records would be moved from Tibet into the Andes. What about that temple in the Andes? Inside an undisclosed, vast cavern there are Temples of Records, Crypts of Records. This cavern is part of a monastery, mostly underground, and is not a temple, but an abbey. Many people have traveled to the Andes in unsuccessful attempts to find this abbey. It's like Shangri-La with impassable barriers, snow and icy peaks — and then in their midst is this valley of summer, this abbey. It, too, will be found when divine forces decree it shall be so. At this time there are Records still in Tibet, in the Andes, and, of course, don't forget Egypt.

QUESTION: During your Mystical Journey to sacred places where the Blessed Virgin has appeared, you visited Fatima, in Portugal. While you were conducting the Fire Initiation at Fatima, the cross fell from your rosary. You told us it was symbolic of a mystical happening that would be occurring among many New Age seekers and initiates. I kept waiting through the months ahead for my cross to fall, but it never did. What does this mean? Does it mean that those whose crosses fell are special in some kind of mystical way that the rest of us do not understand?

ANSWER: No, those for whom the crosses fell were not special in any particular way, any more than the rest of the initiates. It only means that they live in strategic places around the planet where the new established Ley lines are being activated. These initiates occupy a magnetic spot on the planet — at points where several Ley lines connect and increase the electromagnetism of the Divine Force. Those initiates whose crosses fell were simply chosen as instruments through which the Forces were activating that particular location on the planet. You see, the tours taken by so many of us were for the purpose of reestablishing the cosmic currents around the planet linking the great monuments, pyramids and temples together as they were in ages gone by.

The new Ley lines need to be established so that the planet can again become the activated magnet it once was. Those whose crosses fell happened to be occupying an important location. Their crosses fell, symbolic of the reactivated lines of Force. If yours did not fall, not to worry. You, too, are special. Your cross still may fall someday when you happen to be in a very special location, absorbing the currents of the reactivated lines of Force. This reactivation and recharging is taking place now all over the planet.

The crystals and the scarabs given at our Fire Initiations, and the rosaries many of us now use are actually rods of power to help in this planetary undertaking.

My cross fell as a symbol for the initiates of the New Age all over the world. It was a signal that the cross attached to our rosaries was replaced with an unseen symbol of triumph and resurrection — a signal that the Forces of the New Age have now gained such momentum that the resurrection, or rebirth, of the human race is appearing on the distant horizon.

Chapter II

Spiritual Seeking

QUESTION: Some seekers say they have had spiritual experiences through the use of drugs. How can drugs induce spiritual effects? Can some drugs enhance spiritual growth?

ANSWER: Some teachers of esoteric science, while seemingly well-trained themselves, have chosen an undisciplined approach through drugs, and in so doing have attracted numbers of followers who are also seeking to use this method as a kind of short cut to spiritual enlightenment. In analyzing the effect of drugs upon the body, it is not difficult to understand that they could, indeed, induce clairvoyance. However, to be guided to use this method by a spiritual teacher can create untold havoc in the lives of some of their followers and reveals a profound ignorance, or a cruel indifference to the well-being of their disciples.

In the Yoga Sutra teachings of India's renowned Master Yogi Patanjali, he revealed that there were several methods by which the negative spinal chakras might be unsealed, but he made it quite clear that he favored only the method of contemplation and pranayana, or breath control. In the final analysis, this is the method recommended to all spiritual seekers through some form of yoga, which opens only the head centers, the positive force centers.

The seeker will recall that we have spoken of the involuntary clairvoyance which was so prominently developed in the lifewave of the early fourth root race, during the ancient Lemurian epoch. This was the uncontrolled clairvoyance over which souls had no jurisdiction, and which opened them unmercifully to influences of the astral plane, particularly the lower zones. This clairvoyance was activated by and through their overstimulated sympathetic nervous system. The sympathetic nervous system was then, and is now, active in the negative chakras in the spine.

Again, the drug method is that which reawakens the sympathetic nervous system to astral impressions. The use of drugs in invoking psychic powers is to be avoided since it only stirs into activity the negative currents of the sympathetic system which, in the majority of humans, even at this stage of its evolutionary progress, is more in tune with the lower astral than with the higher spiritual planes. It is unwise to stimulate these baser tendencies which were so powerful and predominant in lifeforms during the earlier ages. It is exactly these currents and karmic images in the bloodstream which we are now attempting to overcome, and it is not wise to arouse and give energy to them through the use of drugs.

There are, however, certain herbal and plant concoctions once employed by adept Teachers only during initiation ceremonies in the Mystery Schools which released the higher potential of and aided the initiate in attaining some degree of superconsciousness. Peyote was, and is even now, chewed by certain Native Americans for this purpose — but only during religious and initiation ceremonies. Peyote is a small, spineless cactus whose button-like tops are chewed for hallucinogenic effects. The sacred mushroom is used even now to experience psychedelic visions. Both of these can be dangerous in the hands

Spiritual Seeking

of the unschooled, or when used to excess. Native Americans used them only under the direction of their medicine people during ceremonial activities. It must be realized that any kind of drug, herbal or otherwise, does *not* create any degree of permanent spiritual growth. They only open the consciousness to temporary hallucinogenic visions.

Marvelous herbal concoctions such as the soma drink were employed for beneficent purposes in the Mystery Schools, and by means of them many candidates entered higher levels of consciousness and, through these levels, gained their higher initiations. Again, they were administered only by the hierophant directing the ceremony.

That to which we voice our objections are the drug methods used by those of the dark forces. For instance, opium and heroin most surely open the lower psychic centers, allowing the most vicious and undesirable connections to be established between the carnal nature of the operator and the lower astral plane. This often brings ill health, disaster, misery and mental destruction upon the unfortunate victim once it has its obsessive control over the sympathetic nervous system. LSD, cocaine and other mind altering drugs can also be deadly, leading not only to spiritual, but physical and emotional destruction. The best way to pursue your own spiritual growth is through daily spiritual practice such as meditation or yoga, through spiritual study, through acts of service to others, and through practicing forgiveness.

QUESTION: How should I proceed to share my knowledge of Ancient Wisdom with my friends and loved ones? I long so desperately for those I love to embrace the truths I have found.

ANSWER: No attempt should be made to convince or coerce the skeptic until, or unless, an interest is shown in the subject. Actually, one's own overzealousness may be the very blocking irritant that sidetracks the investigations of others. Only when a friend or loved one evidences a curiosity, and begins to seek the answers to questions, should the believer make an effort to guide another toward an understanding.

Bring up the subject and express your own interest, but unless questions are asked, or interest shown, it is far better to allow individuals to concentrate their attention and efforts upon the purely material problems which lie within the scope of one's capabilities. Individuals tend to build barriers or limitations around their consciousness, and until some of these limitations of perception are removed, another's awareness may be too limited to understand your truth.

Usually one seeks toward the psychic and the mystical only through personal experience. It could be useful to leave mystical literature or New Age books in their reach, so that through curiosity they may choose to read them, and thus open the way to asking further questions. But unless one shows an interest when the subject is discussed, pressing them toward acceptance may tend only to drive them farther away. Let temperance be your guide. Observe their reaction and proceed accordingly when the subject is mentioned.

QUESTION: Can you tell generally about the law of detachment versus commitment to personal missions? How tight is too tight to hold on?

ANSWER: Whenever you make a commitment to higher forces, you automatically become detached from the "things" of Earth. Detachment means you try to make no more unpleasant karma. You cannot serve two Masters. Once you make a commitment to your own spiritual growth, or to your own High Self, material "things" down here become less important. That does not mean you cannot have a commitment or a mission down here.

Robert and I have had a commitment to spiritual growth and teaching since 1951. But there's always some goal ahead down here to be completed — some project to be committed to — total commitment. But we are committed in a detached way because we know that the service is in the etheric form. It's helping you and you and you — and you helping us. That's all etheric, but that's commitment — total commitment.

But once you make your commitment to the world of divine spirit you notice that your heart is no longer attached to this plane because the closer you get to Them, the less attached you will be to things down here.

Once you grasp a vision of heaven, your Earth mission will usually be more easily fulfilled. You live as long as necessary to fulfill the mission you've been sent to do — waiting patiently to grasp the heavenly commitment. But once committed to those Overthere, you will see how your commitment down here will change for the better. Your commitment down here — with detachment — will be more fulfilled and fulfilling.

QUESTION: What is the spiritual, not physical, cause of Alzheimer's disease? Although the body is still functioning, the mind is gone.

ANSWER: The spiritual? If Alzheimer's had not happened, something else of a similar nature may have happened to that person, because of karma. So in that sense, it did not happen by accident. If they are meant not to have it, if the seed atom in the heart does not agree with that particular type of karma, they'll get well. If the karma continues, the soul is meeting a karmic indebtedness and leveling the debt so that the karmic record can be "made straight." There are no karmic accidents.

Difficult as this, or any other physical condition is, it could be that the soul is using this condition as a way to erase some past negative karma. It also could be that the caregiver's karma comes into play, as well. Those caring for one who is ill may be creating positive karma for themselves, or may be paying back a karmic debt owed to the person who is afflicted.

QUESTION: What are the fundamental characteristics of the mystic which I can aspire to achieve?

ANSWER: I would say that the qualities of purity, love and truth best express the characteristics of the mystic. The true mystic should reveal these qualities in his or her life.

To attain purity, the mystic should strive to purify his or her personality — the physical, emotional and mental bodies. First, the physical by right and clean living and by self-control, abstaining from foods and drinks which contaminate and overstimulate the senses, using moderation in catering to the needs of the physical body. This will raise the vibrations of the physical atoms and build a foundation of great resistance, endurance and strength — vitality.

Then one should purify one's emotional body by learning to positively experience and express all emotions, learning the lessons they carry, freeing oneself from the dominion of the lower force centers and transmuting all these emotions into higher forces. Purification of emotion from all its gross and crude elements which require violent vibrations is as important to the mystic as the purification of chemical elements to the alchemist in the work of transmuting one element into another. This will change the vibration of one's astral body, which will become more subtle, pure and beautiful.

As coal is transmuted into diamonds by the process of purification and rearrangement of atoms, so the purified astral body of a mystic will gradually become more and more transparent and luminous, radiating light, joy and serenity, and spreading happiness and peace to those who come under the influence of his or her magnetic field.

Purification of the mental body means stilling the mind to reflect the Higher Self. It means having full control over the emotional and physical bodies. It means transmutation of the concrete mind into the abstract mind, or the mind of the lower personality into the mind of the Oversoul. It means controlling the lower personality and its illusions along with the lower mind. It means consciously raising the pitch of personality to that of the Oversoul, or tuning the rays of one's lower personality to the rays of the Oversoul. It means adjusting our entire conduct, so that instead of self-gratification only, we seek to serve humankind's highest goals, identifying ourselves with divine law and consciously assisting evolution.

After the mystic attains this state, the words of Christ that "the pure in heart shall see God" become a reality. You become one with the Higher Self. But that does not end the work of purification for you, for you have now to take the next step, that of purifying the soul as the transmutation of your soul into Spirit.

Love is the quality of the second aspect of divinity, that of love-wisdom which sees the One beneath the many, drawing the many into union. It is the connecting link between pure Spirit and matter, the positive and the negative, the male and the female principle in the manifested universe. It is the harmonious vibration of the form with the central life — the soul. It is the attractive energy, which builds and perfects the form and makes it a better expression of the Indwelling Energy. It is the motivating power, the incentive of all manifestation.

Love is an emotion which seeks gradual expansion of the self towards the High Self. Love in those who have only experienced a little divine light manifests itself as animal passion. Then on the steps of evolution it shows itself as the love of mate, the love of family, the love of associations, the love of country and, finally, the love of humanity and of God.

The very essence of love is the realization of the union of all Selves. God is love, because, as the One Self, God is all Selves. It is by this realization that the mystic attains to the higher (cosmic) consciousness.

Love is also the great catalytic force which aids in the transmutation of the lower self into the spiritual Self. In the process of this transmutation, powerful spiritual energies are liberated as atomic forces are released in the transmutation of elements, with which spiritual forces flood the universe and help humankind in its march toward godhood.

Truth is the quality of the third aspect of divinity, that of matter or form. It is the recognition and revelation of the Reality, which lies behind all forms. It is the realization of the essence of all facts visible and invisible, on all planes. The revelation of Reality depends on gradual perfecting of all forms. Truth is revealed to each soul according to that soul's capacity to understand, and its effort to receive. For Truth has many aspects and different souls look at Truth from different angles. Some see more of Truth than others because, with an open mind and without any prejudice, they have prepared themselves to receive.

The recognition of Reality is gradual, like a ladder with an infinite number of steps. Those who have found Truth today may abandon it tomorrow after they have found a still higher Truth. Nature reveals her secrets little by little and to those who see, or who are in love with her, to whoever knocks, the door will be opened. Revelation will follow revelation. There is no final Truth, as Truth is eternal.

In the world of separation we stand outside and see the Sun of Truth through our own ray. Someday, when we become one with God, we shall be standing in the center of the Sun and we shall see all rays.

Truth reveals Love through Purity. Love is God, therefore Truth reveals God. It reveals God within and without. And the more we purify ourselves, the more we reveal the divinity within us.

By thus becoming one with the world consciousness, you do not lose your individuality, but will experience individuality and world consciousness simultaneously, and will be able to merge with the mass consciousness of the world.

In the state of samadhi, the yogi is in a trance, but the mind is fully conscious of the Self. When the mind returns to the body with the experience it has had in the superphysical state, one remembers everything.

The Christian doctrine of the at-one-ment, and the teaching of yoga are the same. The Christian mystic speaks of union as at-one-ment and of salvation from sin. The Hindu seeker speaks of Raja Yoga, and of liberation from the lower self. The Jewish mystic will seek total alignment through the Kabbalah. In each case it is the mind that consciously unites the soul with its God, as the Christian calls it, or the lower self with the High Self of the Hindu, or the lower self with the Ain of the Jew. The lower self comes under control of the High Self and the personality and the soul function as a unity, as a coordinated whole, expressing the will of the Inner God.

When an individual can consciously achieve union with the Divine, he or she will lose all sense of separateness. You will not judge anyone. You will see God made manifest in all, and you will see each person as part of yourself. When you see a sinner you will see the sinner in yourself—otherwise you would not be able to see his or her sins. This will be true not only for human beings but for animals and all aspects of the kingdom of God. You will see only good in everything. You will live the life of universal familyhood. You will be a true mystic.

QUESTION: What is the difference between a mystic and an occultist? Do they have the same goals? The same ideals? The same characteristics?

ANSWER: Mysticism is an art of acquiring faculties through which it is possible to have glimpses into the superphysical world, or the God-Self within.

Occultism is an esoteric science, the object of which is to find the laws of the spiritual world, or God (in outer manifestation) by the methods of science and philosophy.

The mystic is the younger sibling of the occultist only in a scientific sense. S/he is not necessarily an occultist, having little interest in methods of science. But the occultist often is a mystic. After initiation, the mystic is merged in the occultist, for s/he has become a student of occult laws and learned to master all forms of manifestation. The mystic achieves that which occultists should regard as their relative goal. A mystic is one

Spiritual Seeking 229

who has experienced God, while the occultist may have done so only on the mental plane.

The mystic follows the path of love and devotion, and enters into full possession of his or her inner life. Having gained realization of his/her new realms of consciousness, the mystic becomes aware of new faculties and finds enlightenment. In this way s/he learns of the innermost nature of the soul and becomes atone with God.

The occultist, endowed with intuition and synthesis, works along the line of will, and seeks to penetrate the hidden depths of nature by recognition of the law in operation and by the wielding of the law which binds matter and conforms it to the needs of the indwelling life, arrives at those intelligences who work with the law, till s/he attains the fundamental intelligence him/herself.

The mystic deals with the evolving life, and will concentrate on abstractions, on the inner life more than the concrete. The mystic is in love with God, and aspires to leap from the place of the emotions to that of intuition.

The occultist deals with the form through which God manifests, rather than God, the divine being. The occultist concentrates attention on the energy, life, force, spirit manifested by forms which veil the Self, and eliminating the veil sheath by sheath, by conscious knowledge arrives at the Self, or form, and with the Creator becomes one.

The mystic is generally compassionate, self-sacrificing and prone to martyrdom. S/he may be a dreamer, a visionary, impractical, emotional, lacking discrimination, and may be of poor health, neglecting the physical needs of the body.

The occultist is generally self-possessed, a person of will and strong principles. S/he is practical, and knows how to discriminate between the real and the unreal, the important and the unimportant. The occultist is healthy, taking good care of the physical body, and may also be selfish, proud and eager for power.

Before becoming an initiate, the mystic must be an occultist and possess the characteristics of an occultist. On the other hand, before the occultist can be trusted with the Secret of the Path, selfishness and pride must be uprooted from his or her life. In other words, the paths of the mystic and the occultist must merge. The heart and the head must work together, and they must both possess the same qualifications.

QUESTION: What is the spiritual purpose of persons being born either mentally impaired or becoming mentally impaired through some type of mishap after birth?

ANSWER: First of all, my Teacher says there is no such thing as an accident. There are some life patterns which are preordained — and only the Lords of Karma understand it. This is where rebirth — reincarnation — answers many questions. Each soul is faced with individual responsibility and individual karmic patterns. Each soul has lived many lives on Earth and has returned to learn more lessons — to pay the karmic debts created in other lives.

One soul might be very young on its path of evolution while another might be older and more evolved. A new physical form and a new personality are assumed by the soul, each adapted to its own needs in order to afford it new opportunities for further growth and development.

Since there is so much involved, the answer to one puzzle often leads to more profound questions. I'm sure the mentally-challenged child, or his or her Guardian Angel, chose a life of such experience, and was attracted to its father or mother's aura. Therefore, the parents of such a child are selected for a very important lesson to be learned, or a karmic debt to be paid. For those experiencing autism, for instance, an entire family may be involved, as well as the afflicted child, in the entire karmic pattern.

As for becoming mentally impaired through some type of mishap after birth, this too must be chosen before reincarnating as a way of spiritual development, or of living at least a partial lifetime of karmic indebtedness. This statement about paying a karmic debt is not meant to sound blaming of the victim. It is meant simply to help us understand why challenging or difficult things sometimes happen to truly good people. They may be paying off some karmic debt, or they may have chosen this path to learn some life or soul lesson.

Until the entire concept of rebirth and karma is better understood by the human race, such questions can't be fully answered. And even then, little understood. For who can understand "the ways of God?"

QUESTION: Explain the cosmic loneliness you write about.

ANSWER: Loneliness is experienced only by the soul who has not learned how to turn within and find the Master. Being turned outward in one's thoughts, one is always lonely in life. To assuage such loneliness, one attempts to make someone else his or her own. But sooner or later must come the realization that no one belongs to another. The sooner the soul begins to realize this, the better, for only when this realization becomes obvious does the soul actually begin the search for something eternal to which it can belong, and which belongs to it.

There is only one someone who is really ours forever, and that is the Heavenly Father/Mother. They are the eternal substance of our being. Once we realize this, our true search for belonging begins, and one is never really lonely again, except in a cosmic sense. Once the soul begins its journey toward the Light of Illumination, the cosmic loneliness begins — the longing to merge with the High Self; the yearning for Self-illumination; the longing to return to the Source from which the soul descended to Earth in rebirth.

QUESTION: I'm not quite clear what is meant by individualization. I know it has much to do with when and how we became individualized souls, but can you explain further?

ANSWER: First, visualize the causal body — the body into which all your good deeds and thoughts have been poured during all your various incarnations — it's called "the house not made by hands, eternal in the heavens"; the house "built without the sound of hammer." When your causal body is at last completed, after many incarnations, it has then become a fit vessel into which the downpouring radiance of the Monad may be received.

A Monad is a unit of consciousness, a fragment of the Universal Consciousness, separated off as an individual entity — a spirit, veiled in the rarest sheath of matter.

This individual entity manifests itself in the celestial realms and projects bodies from itself onto the lower plane. This is an involuntary process. Once this process is over, then the evolution of consciousness begins by contacts received from the physical plane. Many of these entities are gathered together and form themselves into Group Souls, which divide and subdivide themselves until one form is left, possessing its own envelope. Thus is a causal body formed into which the downpouring of the Monadic life occurs.

At first this baby Monad has no sense of others, no self-consciousness. It has simply the will to live, striving after further manifestations of life. Then the great beings, called the Creative Orders, arouse it to "outer" life. A dim sense of "others" arises and self-consciousness is born. The individual becomes aware of I-ness.

Incarnation after incarnation occurs with only the good, the pure and the beautiful of each life being deposited into the bubble of the causal body. Once it attains perfection, this soul is freed from rebirth in the physical realm and becomes omniscient, as a part of the Universal Consciousness. This individualized soul can then manipulate — or travel — through the vibrations of all the spiritual planes.

QUESTION: Do you believe in predestination? If so, how can one change one's life during this lifetime? How does karma relate to freewill?

ANSWER: There are millions of changing atoms in this body, but there are three permanent seed atoms. One, the mental seed atom, is located in the pineal gland. Another is in the heart, called the heart seed atom, and another is in the solar plexus. This one is the emotional seed atom, which records all the emotions we experience, making a cosmic book of judgment.

The mental and emotional seed atoms are related. Both are also related to free will. Through free will you are in control of your thoughts, no one can force you to think in a certain way.

Free will allows you to change your mind — "... be ye transformed by the renewing of your mind." (Rom. 12:2)

Through the use of free will it is possible to change mental and emotional atoms at any time. You can think high thoughts, or you can think low thoughts, which register in the mental seed atom. High or low, they fluctuate like a thermometer going up and down.

The heart seed atom is the one tying you to your fate and your destiny — your past and present karma. The one on which you have recorded your activities here, which unwind like a little movie, with all the karmic picture images you have created pouring out into your bloodstream all the time. So you are the victim, or the beneficiary, of your karma.

Now, the mass of humans has no knowledge of these seed atoms, or that through them they can alter both the influence and type of karma which prevails. You are affected by your karma from this heart seed atom constantly pouring picture images into your bloodstream. At the same time you've got these other two atoms that tie you to free will. Now once you find out about these atoms, you decide they are not going to dominate you. You're going to love so much, you're going to be filled with so much light, that you're going to overcome the record of karma in the heart atom.

So one atom holds us to our fate and our destiny, and two atoms allow us to overcome negative karma through free will and choice. So there is your answer. If we don't know about these two freewill atoms, we succumb to our outpouring karma. But if you find out about these two seed atoms, you are much more in control. That's the free will.

QUESTION: But don't you always have to pay your karma?

ANSWER: Yes, if you submit to it and say, "It's there, so I must accept it." But not if you say, "The karma is there, but I can overcome it if I turn to the light of love and service." By so doing, you'll never have to face that karma, not because you didn't deserve it, but because you were so busy overcoming it. Light always overcomes darkness. Light is always more powerful than darkness. And you can overcome your karma by doing good. Overcome negative karma with better karma. But this cannot be accomplished if you believe that there's nothing to be done because it's simply your karma.

Now there are some types of karma you cannot overcome. Let's say that before my rebirth, a celestial guide says to me, "You have to go back. You did enough bad that it's going to require at least four different lifetimes to balance your karma. Do you want to experience it all in on incarnation, or do you want portions of it doled out over the next four incarnations?" How am I going to handle this?

And my guide is going to say, "You can have it either way." You're going to say, "Guardian Angel, let me have it all in one lifetime. Let me go down into rebirth blind, for example, or crippled." I'll come in afflicted in some way, and I will have accepted this. It doesn't matter how many healers I contact or prayers of, "O God, let me overcome this." I will have taken this karma on, and there is no healer that can heal me.

Let's say I've lived forty years with this affliction. If I have accepted my karma and have paid my debt, perhaps now the slate has been wiped clean. If so, my Oversoul will suddenly say, "Ah, this little soul has lived forty years of this, it's time she was healed. She has paid her karma." I contact a healer again and what happens? All of a sudden I'm healed and think, "Oh God, I've had this for so long, thank you God, I'm healed."

Or perhaps you journey to Lourdes, and you're healed after bathing in the sacred waters. Fifty thousand others go to Lourdes who aren't healed. But here comes this one who has suffered so long and all of a sudden her dreadful karma is lifted. The karma is paid and it's time it was released. And the Oversoul says, "Go into the light, little one, you've paid your karma, you've lived enough of this. Go now and sin no more" — or create no more bad karma. This is why some experience an instantaneous healing at Lourdes. Have you ever seen an instantaneous healing there? Others will return home and say, "I was not healed and I have such faith, why? Why couldn't I?" Well, it wasn't time.

Now when the Blessed Mother appeared to four little children at Garabandal, Spain, many of their neighbors would say, "Conchita, when the Mother comes, ask her to heal me." When the Mother appeared, Conchita would say, "Oh Mother, my neighbor asks may he receive a healing? There are fourteen people here, please will you heal them?" And Mother would say, "I will heal this one, but I will not heal that one. But you tell that neighbor of yours that if he will say the rosary, I will heal him within a year's time. It will take a lot of rosaries, but if he'll do it, I'll heal him." But she wouldn't simply heal everyone instantaneously. She knew exactly who to heal, and who had additional negative karma to overcome.

Now, when I perform healing, I don't do anything but pray. I just open my heart and my consciousness, and let the force flow. Now, I've had instantaneous healings happen. But they are rare. Usually, someone will write me a week later and say, "I never felt anything during the service, but when I reached home I realized I wasn't in pain anymore." Or, "I went to my doctor and he said, 'Your heart is normal' " or, "You don't have diabetes anymore!' " It may be a gradual healing where you're

Spiritual Seeking

taken by surprise — not a sudden obvious action. Instantaneous healings are extremely rare. Even at Lourdes it's a rare happening. Anyway, I never know when healings will occur. Some will be healed, some may be partially healed, some not at all. I have nothing to say or do about it. I just stand and wait like a channel and let the healing energy flow. All I do is pray.

In Closing

Dear Reader,

Thank you for your interest in this book. It would never have been written but for all those seekers who attended my seminars through the years. The personal contact, meeting each one, was wonderful. Thanks to all of you for your questions, for your interest, for your prayers and for your seeking.

Thanks also to my teachers and angels who inspired every answer.

Peace, love and light to all of you, always.

                                          Dr. Earlyne Chaney

Epilogue

Dear Reader,

At the completion of this remarkable book, we want to let you know that just before dawn on the morning of Friday, May 23, 1997, its author, Earlyne Chaney, put aside the body through which she expressed herself for over 80 years. We, her husband and daughter, were both with her at home and shared the peaceful transition.

Many hours of her days and nights were devoted to serving as a teacher and healer for members of Astara, the mystical organization which she co-founded in 1951, and for others around the world. She radiated the love and understanding which came from living the teachings about which she wrote, and up to the very last moments of her life was expressing her love for Astarians, and for all spiritual seekers.

She asked us to convey to all of you who read her Lessons and books that her love, support and healing will continue even more strongly from the realms of Light. We hope you have received strength and wisdom from this, the final book on which she worked while here on this earthly plane.

— Sita and Robert Chaney